COMMUNICATING WITH STUDENTS IN SCHOOLS

A Workbook for Practitioners
and Teachers in Training,
Revised Edition

Richard R. Burke
Bowling Green State University

UNIVERSITY
PRESS OF
AMERICA

LANHAM • NEW YORK • LONDON

Copyright © 1984 by

University Press of America,® Inc.

4720 Boston Way
Lanham, MD 20706

3 Henrietta Street
London WC2E 8LU England

Printed in the United States of America

British Cataloging in Publication Information Available

Library of Congress Cataloging in Publication Data

Burke, Richard R.
  Communicating with students in schools.

  Includes bibliographies.
    1. Teacher-student relationships. 2. Interaction
analysis in education. 3. Child psychology. 4. Oral
communication. I. Title.
LB1033.B87   1984   371.1'02   84-3606
ISBN 0-8191-3878-9 (pbk. : alk. paper)

All University Press of America books are produced on acid-free
paper which exceeds the minimum standards set by the National
Historical Publication and Records Commission.

For Michael, Maureen, and Paul
who are kind enough to expect
less than perfection from my
communication skills.

I wish to extend my appreciation to the many students who commented on the early manuscripts and to Mrs. Judy Maxey, Ms. Sue Boxley and Mrs. Lory Pratt for their assistance in preparation of the manuscript.

CONTENTS

UNIT ONE
Introduction

"Everyone talks about the weather but no one does anything about it." All of us have heard that expression countless times. It is, of course, ridiculously true--no one can do anything about the weather (except learn to enjoy whatever it brings). But we might coin a similar expression: Everyone talks about communication, but no one does anything about it. We hear this all the time:

"A good marriage is based on communication."

"The key to being an effective parent is communication."

A bumper sticker even proclaimed it: "Communication is vital to life." And this, too, is ridiculously true. How could we live without communicating? How could we teach without communicating?

If you have ever been left alone with a deaf and mute or partially mute person, you may remember how you had to begin struggling frantically for some way to communicate. Indeed, communication is vital to life. A painful, usually unbearable, punishment often inflicted by groups on one of their wayward members is called "the silent treatment." Everyone is instructed to avoid all communication with the victim. He is neither spoken to nor heard. While this punishment may seem quite light, in actuality this "silent treatment" is devastating.

It is rather well known among psychologists and physicians that infants thrive on communication as much as milk. Many years ago the psychoanalyst, Rene Spitz (1945), described how infants waste away in institutions primarily because of a deficiency of human interaction and communication directed to the child (not a deficiency of nutrition, but interaction). Yes, the bumper sticker was right--both figuratively and literally--communication is vital to life.

1

Then it follows that the <u>quality</u> of communication one experiences is related to the quality of life one experiences. Research on communication patterns in families bears this out. Professor Burton White (1979) of Harvard University has reported that the amount and quality of language directed to the young child relates strongly to the level of competence that child exhibits later.

Family therapy described in books by Virginia Satir (1967) and others attempts to correct problems of families by correcting their <u>communication</u> patterns. A basic principle of family effectiveness is based upon effective communication patterns within the family.

When a marriage begins to fail the partners often engage the services of a psychotherapist for marriage counseling. What is the special tool of the psychotherapist? You guessed it, <u>communication</u>. People often wonder how "just talking" helps in psychotherapy. The explanation lies in the very special and highly skilled communication patterns the psychotherapist employs. Ineffective communication in families produces significant problems. Correcting these problems logically then requires the very skilled communication patterns of a psychotherapist. Effective communication is the <u>tool</u> of the psychotherapist.

And, just as certainly, effective communication is the <u>tool</u> of a teacher. How could anyone teach without communicating? And how could anyone teach <u>effectively</u> without communicating effectively? Yet, we seldom pause to analyze the quality and effects of our communication. Imagine for a moment the different effect each of the following remarks would have on a student in an art class who is beginning to decorate his face with the paint intended for his canvas:

- "Peter, when are you going to grow up!"

2

- "That's just what I'd expect of you, Peter."
- "Look out, everyone, Peter's putting on the war paint."
- "Peter, have you decided what you're going to put on that canvas?"

Each of these remarks carries a particular, unspoken message to the student, and each remark is likely to have a different effect upon the student's behavior. In a similar situation an art teacher told the student, "Stop being so stupid." The effect of that remark was observed clearly when the student responded, "You're stupid." The student was suspended from the class for three days. We do not mean to excuse the student's behavior, but the response was not without its stimulus.

In his book, Between Parent and Child, Haim Ginott (1965) offered the following illustration of the differential effects of varied communication patterns as related by a group leader and the group members:

> Leader: Suppose it is one of those mornings when everything seems to go wrong. The telephone rings, the baby cries, and before you know it, the toast is burnt. Your husband looks over the toaster and says: "My God! When will you learn to make toast?!" What is your reaction?
>
> Mrs. A: I would throw the toast in his face!
>
> Mrs. B: I would say, "Fix your own damn toast!"
>
> Mrs. C: I would be so hurt I could only cry.
>
> Leader: What would your husband's words make you feel toward him?
>
> Parents: Anger, hate, resentment.
>
> Leader: Would it be easy for you to fix another batch of toast?

3

Mrs. A: Only if I could put some poison in it!

Leader: And when he left for work, would it be easy to clean up the house?

Mrs. A: No, the whole day would be ruined.

Leader: Suppose that the situation is the same: the toast is burnt but your husband, looking over the situation, says, "Gee, honey, it's a rough morning for you--the baby, the phone, and now the toast."

Mrs. A: I would drop dead if my husband said that to me!

Mrs. B: I would feel wonderful!

Mrs. C: I would feel so good I would hug him and kiss him.

Leader: Why?--that baby is still crying and the toast is still burnt?

Parents: That wouldn't matter.

Leader: What would make the difference?

Mrs. B: You feel kind of grateful that he didn't criticize you--that he was with you, not against you.

Leader: And when your husband left for work, would it be difficult to clean up the house?

Mrs. C: No! I'd do it with a song. (Ginott, p. 9.)

Yes, the way we communicate with others certainly makes a difference in their response. This often becomes a vicious cycle. A student's negative response to a teacher's unthoughtful stimulus then develops a response in the teacher which is fueled by the two previous exchanges.

1. Teacher: "Stop being so stupid."
2. Student: "You're stupid."

4

3. Teacher: "Get out of here young man. You get down to the office."
4. Student (under his breath): "You can go to *!?#*!?#."

WHY WE COMMUNICATE THE WAY WE DO

A full treatment of the underlying causes of communication patterns is beyond the scope and intent of this workbook. Yet, it is important to realize that the nature of our communication with others is, among other factors, related to (1) our general view of those others, and (2) our respective roles.

OUR VIEW OF OTHERS. Many people have a rather rigid view of human behavior. They believe there is one <u>right</u> way to be. Anyone of a different color is <u>wrong</u>. Anyone of a different religion is wrong. Anyone of a different lifestyle is wrong. Anyone who has a different set of interests is wrong. To a certain extent all of us may be this way. Our language is full of critical expressions: "He's <u>weird</u>." "She's one of <u>those</u>." If one's view of others is quite critical in this sense, then it very likely follows that our communication with others who diverge from our model of "correctness" will be similarly negative.

Many others, however, have a very appreciative view of human variance. They realize that their own interests, religion, lifestyle, etc., are unique to themselves and some others but that other people <u>must</u> have different values and attitudes and ways of living. This attitude of appreciation for human difference is more than tolerance; it is an active <u>regard</u> for uniqueness. Such a person holds very little stereotype or preconceived notion of the way another person should be. Instead, they anticipate learning all about the particular nature of people they come to know. A colorful poster reflected this

5

value: One comic creature was observing another and proclaimed, "I like you, you're different!"

Most of us naturally fall somewhere between these two views. You might give some serious consideration today to analyzing whether you fall more toward the critical view or more toward the appreciative view. The communication patterns you establish with others surely will reflect the general view of others you hold.

At this point your thinking may be helped by responding to the exercise below.

Perception of Youth Scale

The following are a series of statements about children and help they may or may not need. Beside each item there is a blank upon which you can place a number indicating the degree of your agreement or disagreement. Use a scale from 1 to 10 with the lowest numbers representing complete disagreement and the highest numbers representing complete agreement.

_____ 1. Children need considerable guidance in their choice of companions and friends.

_____ 2. Children should have considerable choice in their studies, even in elementary school.

_____ 3. A child belongs to his parents.

_____ 4. When left to their own tastes and preferences, children will generally select what is a good diet for them.

_____ 5. There is a significant difference between adults and children.

_____ 6. Children are intrinsically good.

_____ 7. An adult may be said to be experienced and a child to be inexperienced.

_____ 8. It is possible to allow children to be themselves in school.

In this exercise your general view of children (students) as others may be reflected. If you agreed more with the odd numbered items, your view of children is likely more the "molding/protective/supervisory" view. If you agreed more with the even numbered items your view is more the "let them be/they are good as they are becoming" view. You can find which way you lean by adding all the odd items--1, 3, 5, 7--and dividing by 4; then do the same for the even items. And whichever is the larger number, odds or evens, represents greater agreement.

This exercise is certainly no valid test of your philosophy or general outlook but just an exercise to help you think about your view of these others--young people.

That our view of others has important impacts on the way we communicate with those others has been demonstrated experimentally. Bugenthal and Shennum (1981; cited by Maccoby and Martin, 1983) described a study in which a child trained to be assertive received more respectful communication from adults if the adults viewed children as socially competent. Shyness in the child led to more condescending adult communication if the adult viewed children as having low social competence.

Your view of others, as we indicated earlier, is determined by many complex factors. One is the role you and others hold with respect to each other.

ROLES AFFECT PERCEPTION OF OTHERS. If you are like many people, you would prefer to talk over a personal problem with a friend rather than with a psychologist. Most students prefer to talk over a problem with a trusted teacher than with the school counselor. A very likely reason for avoiding the psychologist or counselor is that we perceive them according to the role they play: professional helper.

7

If you want to learn the extent to which role perceptions affect our outlook and communication patterns with others, try the following. Sit next to someone at the counter of a restaurant (or similar establishment) and strike a conversation with the person near you. After a while slip a few words into the conversation about how you are a priest or nun (or even a teacher). Notice how the relationship suddenly changes. Why? Obviously the other person now views you according to your role.

Everyone in a classroom has a role which influences the way they treat others and are treated by others. One person has the role of teacher and all the others have the role of student (among students there are many roles, too; one may be the class joker--so no one takes him or her seriously; another may be the class leader, so others look to him or her to decide what is proper). These roles are traditionally associated with certain behaviors and expectations and most people find it very comfortable to behave according to role expectations and very uncomfortable deviating from those role expectations. Thus, if you believe that the role of student is to be motivated, respectful, obedient, industrious, etc. then your attitudes toward those who deviate from these characteristics will surely be different from your attitude toward those who behave according to your expectations of that role. Furthermore, your communication pattern toward those "deviants" will be appropo to your attitude. Additionally, your communication patterns will be quite affected by the role you take for yourself as a teacher. A teacher who sees him or herself as controller will communicate primarily to control. The teacher who sees her role as friend will communicate primarily to promote friendship. The teacher who sees himself as dispenser of knowledge will communicate primarily to dispense knowledge, and the teacher who sees his or her role as resource will communicate to aid those who <u>seek</u> his help.

With all the above in mind, it may be very helpful for you to consider today your idea of a student's role and your idea of a teacher's role and how those views will possibly affect your attitude toward others in your classroom and your communication patterns.

Unit References

Ginott, H. <u>Between parent and child</u>. New York: Avon, 1965, 28-29.

Maccoby, E. E., and Martin, John A. Socialization in the context of the family: Parent-child interaction. In Hetherington, M. and Mussen, P. (Eds.), <u>Handbook of psychology vol. 4: socialization, personality, and social development</u>, New York: Wilcy, 1983.

Satir, V. <u>Conjoint family therapy</u>. Palo Alto, Calif.: Science and Behavior, 1967.

Spitz, R. A. Hospitalism: An inquiry into the genesis of psychiatric conditioning in early childhood. In R. S. Eissler, et al. (Eds.), <u>The Psychoanalytic Study of the Child</u> (Vol. 1). New York: International Universities Press, 1945.

White, B., Kaban, B. T., and Attanucci, J. S. <u>The origins of human competence: Final report of the Harvard Pre-School Project</u>. Lexington, Mass.: Lexington Press, 1979.

UNIT TWO
CHILDHOOD AS DENIAL

Childhood is a time for learning, for playing, for exploring, for having fun, and for growing in all the ways children have the potential to grow. It is not this way for all children, however. For many it is a time of lonely hours spent wishing one could make just one single friend. But for all children, one thing is common - they are not full fledged citizens and they do not share the rights, privileges, and responsibilities of the adult world. In many respects, childhood is a time of denial. John Holt (1974), in his book Escape From Childhood, details the various forms of denial experienced by children and the way this denial tends to create a less than desirable climate for growth.

This second class status and frequent denial has inevitably become a part of the language we use with children. It is an often repeated joke that one child or another thought his first name was no, just having heard it every time someone addressed him during his first three years.

"No, Andy, you can't have cookies now."

"No, Julie, don't pull the cat's ears."

"No, Chris, no T.V. after school."

One study has found that two-year olds have their behavior changed against their will (a form of denial) about every six to seven minutes on the average (Minton, Kagan and Levine, 1971). This is, to some degree, a natural part of socializing the child; but we often take it to extremes. One mother became so conscious of how often she was saying no that she devised a never-say-no plan. Instead of saying no so often, she began saying when or what else:

"You can have cookies for dessert, Andy."

"You can pet the cat like this, Julie."

"You can watch T.V. after dinner, Chris."

This mother's plan seems like little more than a different way of denying, but it does serve to illustrate the extent of denial in childhood. Children and adolescents cannot vote, cannot sign contracts, cannot choose where they will live, cannot do much of anything significant without their parents' approval.

Furthermore and perhaps more importantly, a child's basic self is often denied ("Children are to be seen and not heard."). Because children are younger and usually less experienced than adults, we tend to disregard their opinions, we treat them often in terms of their "cuteness," we see them as fickle and as incapable of serious thought, even about their own desires.

"You don't want that train set, Tom; you don't have any place to put it, and you'd play with it for about two weeks and that'd be the end of it."

"You don't want to go to private school, Susan. How could you stand it without any boys around to flirt with."

"You don't want cookies now, Pat; you'll spoil your dinner."

Not only do children so often hear that they don't want what they think they want, but they also frequently hear that they don't feel the way they feel. For example:

A young girl came home from school crying her eyes out.

"What's the matter, dear?" her mother asked.

"Karen (best friend) is moving away and I'll never see her again. It's not fair."

12

"Oh, for heaven's sake," her mother began. "Now stop
crying. I thought you were hurt or something.
Next week you'll probably have some new friend and
you won't even remember Karen."

In others words, the girl's mother was saying, "Oh, you don't
need to feel this way, just think about it and you won't feel
this way at all."

There was also the child whose brother had broken her
favorite toy. "I hate him," she said. Her mother stooped, put
her arm around the girl and said, "You don't hate your brother, you love your brother."

When a child on a playground throws a ball at another too
hard (because the other had been taunting him) and the other
cries and complains, the teacher takes the first boy by the
arm, drags him over to the one who had been taunting and
says, "SAY YOU'RE SORRY." The boy very likely feels great
joy in succeeding at giving the other what he thought he
deserved, and he very likely feels even more negative about
the child now to justify his aggressive behavior. But the
teacher wants him to sincerely express regret.

Teachers and parents who habitually communicate in this
way are in very real ways telling the child that something is
wrong with her self. Hearing constantly that your feelings are
not right or that your preferences are irrational is certain to
result in a confused self-image at best.

Abraham Maslow, one of America's great humanists, wrote
about the self as follows:

> We have, each one of us, an essential inner-nature
> which is intrinsic, given, "natural" and, usually, very
> resistant to change ... no psychological health is possible
> unless this essential core of the person is fundamentally
> accepted, loved, and respected by others and by himself
> ... (Maslow, 1962, pp. 35-36).

Psychotherapist Nathaniel Branden has written eloquently of the denial process and its effect on our personalities. The people he sees in therapy, and millions of others who seek help, suffer from a loss of _self_ - a disowned self. He explains this process convincingly in his book, The Disowned Self (1971):

> We hear more and more today about the fact that many people suffer from a sense of unreality, that they have lost touch with themselves, that too often they do not know what they feel, that they act with numb obliviousness to that which prompts or motivates their actions. The problem is not new, but in recent years it has received an unprecedented amount of discussion and publicity - not only among psychologists and psychiatrists, but among educated people everywhere. Psychotherapists of different schools have developed numerous techniques and methods aimed specifically at bringing people into better touch with themselves and guiding them to experience a more meaningful sense of their own identity (Branden, 1971, p. 3).

Branden goes on to explain how people tend to loose touch with themselves:

> To begin with, many parents teach children to repress their feelings. A little boy falls and hurts himself and is told sternly by his father, "Men don't cry." A little girl expresses anger at her brother, or perhaps shows dislike toward an older relative, and is told by her mother, "It's terrible to feel that way. You don't really feel it." A child bursts into the house, full of joy and excitement and is told by an irritated parent, "What's wrong with you? Why do you make so much noise?" Emotionally remote and inhibited parents tend to produce emotionally remote and inhibited children - not only by the parents' overt communications but also by the example they set; their own behavior announces to the child what is "proper," "appropriate," "socially acceptable" (Branden, 1971, p. 7).

Branden further explains that many feelings, desires, or emotions the child has been taught to think of as bad are quickly disowned. The child no longer even recognizes these feelings, and she is no longer able to sense her own identity. Her identity may become a collection of interests, attitudes, and feelings borrowed from parents or teachers. Thus, the process of alienation and self-repudiation has begun. Giving up his own judgments and feelings for another's, the child learns to disown aspects of his own personality.

This process of denial and self-alienation may begin in childhood, but it certainly continues feverishly through adolescence. These teenage years are when the child is often redoubling her efforts at being herself. Consequently, parents and school personnel may react with intensified denial.

Many teachers, however, practice the art of education in its fullest meaning - with a regard for the child's intellectual, emotional, and physical growth.

Most of us, however, want our children and students to grow up with healthy self-esteem and with a clear sense of self-identity. At the same time, of course, we don't want to spoil them, to give them anything they want at any time. After all, we can't give them everything! But we don't have to destroy their emerging identity in the process of denying what we must deny.

Children learn about themselves, in part, from the feedback they get from others. It is useful here to imagine how it would be to never have seen your reflection. Indeed, most people seem to have difficulty passing a mirror without stealing a glance. But how do we know what our selves look like, what we are all about as a person. In other words, how do we ever come to a sense of identity? Partly, this is a result of what is reflected back to us verbally from parents and teachers. Thus, adults can use language with children that serves as a mirror for the child's self.

THE SKILL--VALUE REFLECTION AND CLARIFICATION. The skill which emerges from these concerns is, "whenever possible take the opportunity to help the child see and hear who he is and what he is all about with language that recognizes and clarifies the child's value--even if you must deny what he wants."

Note the following examples:

A girl wants a popsicle just after her father has dressed her in clean clothes.

"A popsicle! You sure do love popsicles. You can have one when you have clothes on that aren't so clean. I'd bet you'd eat popsicles for every meal, wouldn't you!"

Notice that the father reflected the child's value even though he did not permit the popsicle.

A teenage boy is helping his parents select a new car. He points to a racy sports car and says he thinks they should buy that.

"Boy, I'll bet that's what you'd buy if you had the money, eh?"

Again, this mother makes a point to reflect the boy's value even when she wouldn't accept the idea.

It is important to note that the tone of voice used by these parents is sincere and reflects genuine value recognition, not sarcasm.

EXERCISE: VALUE REFLECTION

For each of the following situations write a response which either denies or permits the student's request but which reflects and clarifies the value the student is expressing.

16

1. A student wants to go to the school library more often than he is permitted, and you cannot allow it.

    _____

    _____

    _____

2. A student wants to use colored pens for work which should be in blue ink.

    _____

    _____

    _____

3. A student wants to know why he can't wear shorts to school. You must follow the school rule.

    _____

    _____

    _____

4. A student wants to have more spelling games. You can arrange this, but still reflect the value.

    _____

    _____

    _____

5. A student wants to bring his pet to school after he already brought the pet twice. You must deny the request (but reflect the value).

_____

_____

_____

FEEDBACK

Expressions which may not be exactly like those which you wrote but which would reflect the skill you practiced would be as follows:

1. "Jill you can go to the library again when it's your turn tomorrow. You just love to work there don't you. Maybe you'll turn out to be a librarian."

2. Pat, I'd like these papers to be done in standard blue or black ink. You can use the colored pens on your practice papers though. You really love to make things look pretty don't you."

3. Tom, our committee decided no shorts until the last week of school. I guess you feel more comfortable in shorts, huh?"

4. "I guess we could have a few more spellings games. I see that you're going to be a real competitor."

5. "Terry, the other children need a chance to bring their pets. You really like to bring your cat. I can see why, he's so pretty."

VALUE REFLECTION <u>AFTER</u> DENIAL. When you need to both deny a student's request and attempt to recognize the value behind that request, it is generally preferable to provide value reflection <u>after</u> the denial.

Examples (value reflection is underlined):

"We had better wait until after lunch for the snack, Joe. <u>You just can't wait can you. You sure love to eat. I'll bet you're going to be a chef some day.</u>"

"Your turn will come soon, Amy. <u>I'll be sure to see you get your turn because I know this is your favorite game.</u>"

When students always hear your reflection of their value before your denial, they will soon come to feel that the value reflection cues the denial and is associated with the denial. That is, they may hear you begin to recognize the value behind their request and say to themselves, "Oh boy, here it comes. I can never do anything." When students regularly hear the value recognition <u>following</u> the denial (appropriately), they first feel the disappointment of the denial and then they feel that you at least have attempted to understand them. They can now say, "He doesn't always let you do what you want, but he seems to understand us."

In the three following situations first deny the student's request and <u>follow</u> the denial with a sincere recognition of the value underlying the request.

1. Students want to have their class outside on the first nice day of spring.

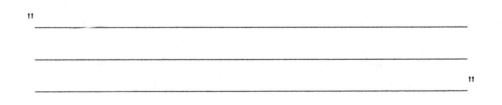

2. A girl wants to be excused from her social studies class after finishing her assigned work to go to the home economics area to work on a project.

"
_____

_____

_____ "

3. A boy asks for just five more minutes at recess when it's time to go into class.

"
_____

_____

_____ "

FEEDBACK

Examples of appropriate responses might be:

1. "The work we have to do requires that we be inside today. I know you love to get out of the building and get into the sunshine. We'll reserve a day for it."

2. "You can work on your home ec. project during your home economics class, Ann. I'd like you to help Bob with his work now. I guess you're really involved with that project, huh? I'd like to see it when you can bring it up some time."

3. Oh, Jeff, come on, you know we have only twenty minutes. You'd increase it to two hours wouldn't you? You'd love to play most of your day, wouldn't you?"

In each of these examples the denial came first and an understanding recognition of value came <u>after</u> the denial.

WON'T REFLECTION OF INAPPROPRIATE VALUES MERELY STRENGTHEN THOSE VALUES?

Many teachers wonder if it isn't wrong to recognize students' inappropriate values in a sincere, appreciative way. Aren't we actually <u>affirming</u> those values; don't we actually approve of them when we verbally reflect an appreciative recognition of them?

It is important to say that in these examples we are not <u>approving</u> the student's values. We are recognizing them, hearing them, acknowledging them. In doing this we are making it unnecessary for the student to press further for recognition of her value. When you call to someone from a distance and you are not heard, what do you do? You raise your voice, you yell louder and louder. Perhaps you also wave your arms. You press harder and harder to make yourself heard, to get something across. And so it often is with needs and values, especially when we are young and it is so hard to get anyone to take us seriously. Showing the student that you hear her and that you hear what she is valuing, sincerely and nonjudgmentally allows the child to tone down the need to press for a particular value and instead to see other points of view. Consider this illustration.

> A young teenage boy was pouting around his house because he had to go with his family to spend a week at his grandparents' house. He had been grim for two days and came to sit in the living room, his arms folded, a scowl on his face. His father noticed.
> "You don't want to go to grandma's do you?"
> "No."
> "You don't have your records and stuff there."
> "No, there's <u>nothin'</u> down there."
> "You get bored there, nothing to do."

"There's <u>never</u> anything to do there."

"All your friends are here."

"Yeah, there's no one I know down there."

"They treat you--well--as though you're a child."

"They think I'm a <u>baby</u>."

"It must be a <u>real</u> <u>drag</u> to spend a week there," the father concluded (with sincerity in his voice).

The boy got up, unfolded his arms, and walked away saying, "Oh, I guess I can make the best of it."

In this example the father was recognizing the boy's values and feelings so thoroughly that the boy had no reason to push for recognition any longer. Very clearly, his message had been heard. The father did not strengthen the negative attitude--he actually helped the boy to be able to see another point of view simply by showing a willingness to hear <u>his</u> felt point of view.

There is some evidence to suggest that simply recognizing and reflecting the student's desire to do something that you must deny enables the student to more cooperatively adhere to the restrictions (Koestner, Ryan, Bernieri, and Holt, 1983). Experimenters gave students a large tablet on which they could paint. There was, however, a margin that they wanted the students to stay away from. Some students were merely told they should not paint over the margin. Other students were told that the experimenter understood how hard it was to keep within the restricted space - and that he knew it would be more fun to paint freely over the margin, but that he wanted them to avoid making a mess. The group that had their probable feelings recognized and reflected painted significantly neater drawings than the groups that had no such understanding communicated.

Many of the exercises in this workbook are built upon this and other research findings: it is generally more effective in the long-run to use requests rather than demands, to keep the pressure low, to give reasons rather than threats, and to communicate a sympathetic understanding when possible (Weber, 1982; Wolfgang & Glickman, 1980).

EXERCISE

For each situation below, communicate an understanding of how the students would rather not be under certain restrictions you must impose:

A. When you set a deadline for a paper to be submitted.

"

_____

_____

_____ "

B. When you request only very quiet talking in the classroom.

"

_____

_____

_____ "

In this section we have been stressing the importance of recognizing and reflecting children's values, preferences, and needs. This may result both in a child with a healthier development of identity and also a more cooperative student. In the next section, we turn to a similar skill applied more to feelings and emotions.

Unit References

Branden, Nathaniel. The disowned self. New York: Bantam, 1971.

Holt, John. Escape from childhood. New York: Ballentine Books, 1974.

Koestner, R., Ryan, R. M., Bernieri, F., and Holt, K. "The effects of controlling versus informational limit setting styles on children's intrinsic motivation and creativity." Unpublished manuscript, Department of Psychology, University of Rochester, 1983.

Maslow, Abraham. "Some basic propositions of growth and self-actualization psychology." In Perceiving, behaving and becoming: 1962 Yearbook of the Association for Supervision and Curriculum Development, pp. 34-39.

Minton, C., Kagan, J., and Levine, J. Maternal control and obedience in the two-year-old. Child Development, Vol. 42, 1971.

Weber, W. A. "Classroom management." In Classroom teaching skills, J. M. Cooper (Ed.). Lexington, Massachusetts: D. C. Heath and Co., 1982.

Wolfgang, C. H. and Glickman, C. D. Solving discipline problems: Strategies for classroom teachers. Boston: Allyn and Bacon, 1980.

UNIT THREE
EMPATHIC UNDERSTANDING

Empathy is a feeling of identification with another's emotion. An individual is experiencing the empathy communicated by another person when he feels understood, heard, as if the other is really in tune with the deeper meanings of his emotion.

The empathic understanding of others is absolutely vital to healthy development. Children in school, especially older children, gradually become social beings and subject to all the important social expectations of their peer groups and society at large. They soon learn that there are particular criteria for being acceptable, and the need to be accepted and valued by others is often the most strongly felt need in life. Most children wonder if they will measure up and fear the worst. Many, perhaps most, carry their fears and anxieties inside, each one thinking he or she is the most despicable, weirdest kid in the school.

In his book, Freedom to Learn, Carl Rogers (1969) talks about the meaning empathy has played in his own life.

> I can testify that when you are in psychological distress
> and someone really hears you without passing judgment on
> you, without trying to take responsibility for you,
> without trying to mold you, it feels damn good. At these
> times, it has relaxed the tension in me. It has per-
> mitted me to bring out the frightening feelings, the
> guilts, the despair, the confusions that have been a part
> of my experience. When I have been listened to and when
> I have been heard I am able to reperceive my world in a
> new way and to go on. It is amazing that feelings which
> were completely awful become bearable when someone
> listens. It is astonishing how elements which seem
> insoluble become soluble when someone hears; how con-
> fusions which seem irremediable turn into relatively
> clear flowing streams when one is understood. I have
> deeply appreciated the times that I have experienced this
> sensitive, empathic, concentrated listening (page 225).

Yet, the language we have learned to use with children is a language of denial:

"Put that down. You don't want that."

"Oh stop crying. Come here, I'll give you something to cry about."

"I'm sure you think this is love, but believe me you'll learn the difference."

"Oh, you don't hate school. You know very well you like it."

These patterns of communication get in the way of empathic understanding and serve only to prevent the child from ever knowing himself well. We communicate so much denial to children, no doubt, because be have come to see childhood as basically a period of denial.

Communicating with empathy requires a desire and ability to put yourself in another's shoes, to gain their perspective. Of course, this requires an awareness on your part that others may indeed have a perspective different from yours'. Many people seem to have no ability to view the perspectives of others as worthy (unless they happen to agree with their own). To Democrats, Republicans are all tight-lipped conservatives and Republicans may feel Democrats are all wide-eyed liberal blockheads; to communists capitalists are greedy exploiters, and to capitalists the Communists are evil agents of the devil.

So a first requirement toward empathic understanding is that you become very aware that your perspective or view of the world is merely one view. Another person looking through their own mental lens sees the world from a different perspective. As one whose chosen career is working with people, this is an essential outlook.

In the next few days it will help you to attempt to hear another's perspective--and to appreciate it--especially when it is not similar to your own perspective.

THE EFFECTS OF EMPATHY

To communicate with empathy is to communicate so that the other person feels genuinely _heard_. She or he might be able to say of you:

"I felt understood."

"He really seemed interested in what it is like to be me."

"She seemed to be able to put her finger on feelings I was only faintly aware of."

Imagine you are listening to the following dialogue as a counselor or teacher expresses empathy:

Student: "Mr. Cartwright is always picking on me."

Counselor: "He's really down on you."

Student: "Every day it's the same thing. If I hand in a paper he complains because it's not finished or something."

Counselor: "Even when you try he finds something wrong."

Student: "He likes all those girls though. They can't do anything wrong. I'd like to see him get it some day."

Counselor: "He's developed a lot of anger in you. It's gotten now so you'd like to see him hurt. If only he would say just one good thing about you. That's all you want."

It would be much more common, of course, for a teacher to respond with statements like these:

"Mr. Cartwright doesn't pick on students for nothing. What are _you_ doing? Do you think he does this for no reason?"

When people experience empathy, however, they are more likely to open themselves to the reality of the situation, to see their part in the exchange.

A boy who was new to a school was wearing his coat to class even though the room was perfectly warm. The teacher approached him at his desk and said quietly, "Pete, I've asked everyone to leave their jackets in their lockers. I guess you have reasons for wearing yours even though it's important to me that we come without coats. I guess you must need it."

"Well," Pete said. "I guess I can leave it. I will tomorrow."

Now this is not what you will hear every time, but it is generally easier for a student to consider another's request when he is being treated with some respect.

NONVERBAL EMPATHY

Communication with empathy is done both verbally and nonverbally. Empathy is communicated nonverbally by showing the other person that you are listening actively. This can be done simply by positioning yourself so as to imply "I'm with you."

This would be reflected by sitting close to the other or leaning toward them, coming out from behind your desk, leaning forward slightly, offering your total attention. Facial expressiveness and eye contact can also communicate empathy.

Thus, in order to make another person feel as if they are really being heard, you would not sit behind a desk nor clean a blackboard, nor straighten your desk, nor walk around it, etc. as they talk to you. You would instead sit close and show with your posture, face and eyes, that you are eager to understand what it is like to be that person.

VERBAL EMPATHY SKILLS

The words and expressions you use add a verbal dimension to your communication. The following types of verbal expression help communicate empathy.

A. <u>Recognition</u>

These are expressions which simply let the other person know you are hearing. Examples:

Mm hmm; I see; yes.

These expressions are inserted into the dialogue occasionally to show the student you are alert to what he is saying.

B. <u>Reflection</u>

These are verbal statements which literally mirror the other's words. Example:

Student: "Oh, she made me do all these stupid exercises that took forever to do."

Teacher: "You thought the exercises were stupid and too lengthy."

C. <u>Translation</u>

Translation means putting the student's words into another form. Examples:

1. Student: "I don't think I could stand to go to college for four years.

Teacher: "For you college would be a drudgery."

2. Student: "Adrian took my pens. I know she did it. She's always taking things and saying she didn't."

Teacher: "You've seen Adrian do this sort of thing before so now you are certain she has done it again."

D. <u>Analogy</u>

The use of analogy enables the student to gain a unique perspective on his thoughts and gives you an opportunity to think harder about just what the student is saying. Example:

    1. Student: "My mother just won't give up. She has to know every little thing I do, everyone I talk to, everywhere I go."

        Teacher: "She's like a rope around your neck getting tighter and tighter."

    2. Student: "Algebra is so dumb, all these symbols and letters. I don't know one from another."

        Teacher: "It's like a foreign language to you. Everyone else in class knows how to speak it, but you don't understand a word."

E. Clarification

These expressions ask the student to explain his thoughts or feelings further. Examples:

    1. Student: "Pete keeps saying I'm not on his team and I know I am."

        Teacher: "I'm not sure I understand, Tom."

    2. Student: "I qualified for the squad but my mother says that if I do it I'll have to give up Scouts and--well, I...I don't want to do it."

        Teacher: "Tell me again, Carol, I'm not sure I have it straight."

F. Feeling Recognition

Frequently you will notice that someone is somewhat emotionally upset but not yet expressing it. A normal reaction is to discourage such expression: "Now, don't cry; it'll be okay, don't worry."

When you help a student recognize and express his feeling you will consequently help him to work through his problem more rationally.

Examples of feeling recognition:

1. Student (distraught): "I...I worked all night on that paper and...and she just threw it in the wastebasket. I even went to the library and... oh, what's the use."

    Teacher: "That really hurt, Karen. You must feel like you're giving up now."

2. Student (near tears): "I don't know what to do. My father wants me to live with him and my mother wants me to...she wants me to live with her."

    Teacher: "This must be tearing you up, Jim... it's okay to cry."

    SPECIAL NOTE: When a student cries it is best to avoid denial expressions such as "don't cry" and avoid trying to cheer them up with expressions such as "it'll be okay, don't worry." It is better to just attempt to recognize the feeling, "You must feel very lost" and possibly touch the student's shoulder, hand the student a tissue and avoid putting your arms around the student. Simply remain quiet and wait for them to go on.

EXERCISE

Now read over the following dialogue between the teacher and student and notice the way the teacher employs these various empathy expressions.

> Teacher (on playground): "Tom, you don't seem to be playing with the other kids today."
>
> Student: "I just don't feel like playing today. None of those kids want to play with me anyway."

Reflection----------Teacher: "Nobody wants to play with you."
(mirror the   Student: "Everytime I ask them if they
student's words)   want to play something, they want to
                             play something else."

Recognition--------Teacher: "I see."
(indicate you hear) Student: "I don't care though, if they
                             don't want to play with me, I won't
                             play with them when they want to."

Translation--------Teacher: "You'll get back at them."
(re-form the   Student: "Yeah, they don't know how
student's words)   to play kick dodge as good as me
                             anyway."

Feeling Recognition-Teacher: "You seem pretty angry, Tom.
(label the feelings   I think it must hurt your feelings
you sense in the   to be left out."
student)   Student (choking up): "I don't like
                             this school."

Clarification-------Teacher: "I'm not sure I understand,
(express a need to   Tom."
hear more)   Student: "Well, I don't have any friends
                             and it's...no fun like where I
                             used to go to school."

Analogy-------------Teacher: "It's like a bad dream for
(compare the   you."
situation to
something similar)

Notice that the teacher didn't give Tom advice ("Oh, just go play, it won't do you any good to just mope around"); and she didn't try to analyze the problem ("Well, what do you do that makes them not want to play with you").

What the teacher did was to use professional communication skills to help the student articulate his problem and his

32

feelings. Now that the student has been <u>heard</u>, he can go on to other things.

EXERCISE

For each of the following situations write the type of expression called for. Before writing your response <u>be sure to refer to the definitions given earlier</u>.

A. Student: "I can't stand Mrs. Paine. She's unfair and mean."

Write a <u>reflection</u> statement to mirror a part of the student's message:

"_____

_____"

B. Student: "I wish I had never taken algebra. I hate it."

Write a <u>translation</u> expression to rephrase the student's message:

"_____

_____"

C. Student: "This school stinks. I can't wait to get out of here."

Write an <u>analogy</u> expression to show you have developed a picture of what the student is conveying:

"_____

_____"

D. Student: "I think I want him to ask me to the dance but I'm not sure if it would be good."
Write a <u>clarification</u> response to get the student to re-phrase her thinking:

"_____

_____ "

E. Student: "I thought I was really going to make the team, I...I put so much work into those practices and...I don't understand it."
Write an expression of <u>feeling recognition</u> to help the student share his <u>feeling</u>:

"_____

_____ "

Recognizing and reflecting feelings is really the essence of these communication skills relating to empathy. Think of the range of feelings people experience: anger, fear, apprehension, conflict, disappointment, joy, expectations, humiliation, sadness, grief, frustration, excitement, boredom, anxiety, rage, etc.

EXERCISE

On the space below each expression, use one word to label the student's feelings or emotions. Use the list offered above, but don't be bound by it.

A. "I don't know how I'll do on this test tomorrow. Maybe I should study more. I hope she doesn't have those stupid fill-in questions."

_____

B.   "This is hard. I don't know what you want us to do. I'll just screw it up anyway."

_____

C.   "I'll get him back. He thinks he's so big and better than anyone else. Just wait."

_____

D.   "I didn't get to go to the dance. My mother said I couldn't because I owed her $10 and I couldn't spend money on a dance until I paid her back. Oh, I wanted to go to that dance so much."

_____

E.   "This class is a drag. I'm not going to be a writer. What do I have to take English for?"

_____

F.   I want to go to St. Stephen's High School but all my friends are going to Central. I don't know..."

_____

Now read the following dialogue between a teacher and student. Whenever you see an empathy skill, label the type of skill used on the blank in the margin.

Student: "Hi, Mr. Evans. Have you seen my brother?"

Teacher: "He was here a while a go, John. How are things with you?"

Student: "Oh, okay. If only I didn't have that stupid gym class."

_____ Teacher: "The gym class is giving you problems?"

Student: "Oh, that new teacher thinks he's so...well, he thinks we're all athletes or something."

_____ Teacher: "Mm hmm."

Student: All he does is yell all the time and tells you how slow you are."

_____ Teacher: "He yells all the time..."

Student: "Well, when he's not acting the big coach."

_____ Teacher: "You seem pretty angry with him, John, maybe a little worried."

Student: "I can't do all that stuff."

_____ Teacher: "Seems maybe like entering basic training for the Army."

Notice that the teacher was not trying to show the student how his attitude was wrong nor how he could overcome his problem nor how his problem was trivial:

"Oh, come on, John, you've got a negative attitude already. You'll never give yourself a chance that way."

36

"You'll feel different later, John. Takes some getting
    used to."

"Now surely you've got more important things to worry
    about than that, John."

The teacher instead was trying to listen to the student, trying
to understand <u>verbally</u> what it feels like to be that student.
He didn't probe, he didn't give advice, he just tried to help
the student to feel very deeply heard. Now that you have
these skills, <u>use</u> <u>them</u>. People everywhere have a need to be
heard and understood if only for a moment--bank tellers,
grocery cashiers, store clerks, cafeteria workers, teachers,
friends--literally everyone can benefit from your attempt to gain
their perspective through these communication skills.

HOW YOU MIGHT BEGIN PRACTICING

Earlier you read that it is necessary to realize that everyone is unique. Everyone has a perspective that is different to
some degree from yours. If you feel that perspectives different
from yours are only to be ridiculed or criticized, then frankly
there is little hope. But if you do realize that there is more
than one valid way to look at something, then you open yourself to human experience and you have the necessary outlook
for helping others.

You can begin with the people nearest you: your room-
mates, friends, parents, brothers and sisters, co-workers.
Instead of being quick to criticize their views or tastes, listen
carefully. Attempt to reflect what you hear. Ask for clarification when you want to hear more.

You can practice <u>feeling</u> <u>recognition</u> wherever you see
someone who obviously is experiencing significant feelings or
who must be--simply because of the situation they are in:

A cashier at the grocery store who looks like she's
about to collapse and who has twelve people lined up

with full carts very obviously must feel some stress. It doesn't take a great deal to imagine how she feels: "Boy, I bet you're ready to go home by now."

A gas station attendant who waits on you in pouring rain: "I imagine these are the kind of days you could give this job to someone else."

The point is that you must practice these skills and allow them to become a part of your natural way of interacting if you expect to have them when you're on the job teaching.

For starters, try the following:

1. The next time you find yourself in an argument or simple difference of opinion with another person, give yourself over to the other's side. Make a gradual, but complete attempt to gain her or his perspective and to lose yours. We are not advocating you become spineless, but we do feel it is necessary to practice losing your perspective as an aid to gaining another's. Below, report the results:

Describe the situation:

_____

_____

Describe the effect on the other person:

_____

_____

_____

2. Watch a television program--soap opera, drama, movie--and attempt to identify the feelings behind the words characters are saying (she must feel as if..., he'd probably like to...).

PROGRAM: _____

DATE: _____

Label and list feelings you guessed at and identified:

_____

_____

_____

3. When you are having a conversation, notice when you begin thinking of what you will say. Most of us listen to only about half of the other's response and then begin forming our own response on the basis of what we heard initially. This indicates how little we are interested in really listening to the other and how important it is to force our own perspective. Try catching yourself when you do this and perhaps even admit it out loud.

What has been the result of this practice?

_____

_____

_____

_____

EDUCATED GUESSING

Much of what you have been doing in your attempts to convey empathy can be termed educated guessing. You pick up subtle cues as to how another must feel and verbalize your guess. This can be useful with individuals or even with groups.

How do you think a new student in a school feels on her first day? _____

How do you think many students feel before an important test?

_____

How do you think a student feels who has been called to the school office and doesn't know why?

_____

The skill involved with educated guessing simply requires you to be sensitive to those times when almost anyone would feel a certain way and to verbalize your understandings--even when the student has shown no signs.

"I imagine you must feel a little anxious today. You don't know your way around or what to expect."

" I know many of you must be a little nervous about this test."

You might say to a student who tells you he has information about a crime in your school: "It must have taken a lot of thought to come to me with this. You must feel a little awkward."

Unit Reference

Rogers, C. Freedom to learn. Columbus, Ohio: Charles Merrill, 1969.

UNIT FOUR
WHEN THINGS GO WRONG

Discipline problems inevitably arise in any classroom. Some classrooms, however, have more than their share and some have far less. What causes the difference? Many factors must be considered. The nature of the students may be different from one class to another or different class "chemistry" may exist among classes. Yet, it may also be that some teachers have the skill to prevent problems from building or to de-escalate problems that have gotten a bit out of hand. These skills, of course, are communication skills.

It is important to state here that a teacher will no doubt have fewer discipline problems if he or she uses the skills covered in the previous unit. So, a part of the trick of creating a good classroom climate is to be a teacher who understands and empathizes with skill. This section addresses the need for effective communication skill when things do go wrong. Unfortunately, this is the very situation when communication skills break down and the teacher tends toward commands and orders, which often makes the situation worse. Teachers are commonly encouraged to avoid threatening statements and to keep their remarks clear, calm, and professional (Howell & Howell, 1979). Several researchers have found that scolding students harshly becomes a very ineffective and problematic strategy (Faust, 1977; Walker, 1979).

Others (Hoffman, in press; Lepper, 1983) have found that children are most likely to internalize behavioral requests of adults when the pressure used by adults is just barely enough to produce the change. Lepper has termed this the "minimal sufficiency principle." Teachers may sometimes find that heavy handed power assertion works well at first, but students are more likely to comply in the long-run (as even when the teacher is not present) when our pressure is minimal.

41

This principle is rather well established, yet it may seem somewhat contrary to our expectations. It seems somewhat natural for a teacher to use strong pressure when he wants an uncooperative student to comply with some rule or request, and it seems somewhat less likely for minimal pressure to work more effectively. This "contrary to expectations" phenomenon resembles that which one understands in the old adage about catching more flies with honey than with vinegar. Many teachers have learned, contrary to their expectations, that they can best get attention by speaking very quietly than by shouting. It is not easy to learn to relax our pressure with children; but, contrary to what seems natural we may more often gain compliance with our requests when we use minimal pressure.

The exercises which follow are all "low key" forms of communication which have been supported by research and by many teachers as highly professional and effective.

SKILL #1: SPEAK TO THE SITUATION, NOT TO THE CHARACTER OR PERSONALITY OF THE STUDENT.

This skill advocated by Ginott (1972) simply requires that you confine your remarks to a student's behavior and to the problem at hand and avoid personal attacks.

Examples of personal attacks:

"Act your age."

"When are you going to grow up."

"Stop acting like a child."

"Is that what you do at home?"

"How can you be so stupid."

"John, I've told you before not to use so much paint. When are you going to grow up."

Speaking to the personality or character of the student is inappropriate for several reasons. First, it tells the student nothing useful about how to correct her behavior. Secondly, it produces emotional resentment in the student and thereby lessens his ability to cooperate. Thirdly, it further damages already weak self-images. Speaking to the situation, on the other hand, is a problem-solving approach:

> "John, you've used too much paint again. You'll need to get some paper towels now."

> "Ann, writing on your desk is inappropriate. Please get some towels and clean your desk now."

EXERCISE:

Indicate with a checkmark which of the following expressions speak to the situation instead of the character of the student.

_____ "Peter, get back in your seat. You're acting like a third-grader."

_____ "Frank, you left the door open. Please remember to close it the next time you come in."

_____ "Carol, put Alan's crayons back in his desk."

_____ "Joe, keep your hands to yourself. Shall we call your parents and let them know about what kind of boy you are?"

_____ "Tom, stop acting like an idiot. Sit down."

_____ "Pat, please come back after class to clean the writing off your desk. Next time, please write on paper."

FEEDBACK

In the situations above, those expressions which were restricted to the situation at hand and the student's behavior were the second, third, and last expressions. The others all included some attack on the student's character.

Now respond to the following situations by writing first a response which _inappropriately_ speaks to the character of the

43

student and second a response which appropriately speaks to the situation only.

1. A girl plays with coins on her desk as you try to teach.

   Negative - speaks to character of the student:

   "
   _____
   _____
   "

   Positive - speaks only to the situation:

   "
   _____
   _____
   "

2. A boy on the playground runs around poking other children.

   Negative - speaks to character of the student:

   "
   _____
   _____
   "

   Positive - speaks only to the situation:

   "
   _____
   _____
   "

3. A boy loiters near a class looking in through the door window as you walk to the office.

   Negative - speaks to character of the student:

   "
   _____
   _____
   "

Positive - speaks only to the situation:

"
_____

_____ "

4. A girl chats with another instead of working on her assignment.
Negative - speaks to character of the student:

"
_____

_____ "

Positive - speaks only to the situation:

"
_____

_____ "

5. A boy allows his coat to fall on the floor after hanging it up and fails to put it back.
Negative - speaks to character of the student:

"
_____

_____ "

Positive - speaks only to the situation:

"
_____

_____ "

FEEDBACK

Some examples of negative responses for the situations above would be similar to those which follow.

"Susan, when are you going to grow up. Put those coins away now and pay attention."

"John, aren't you ever going to learn. Those kids are never going to play with you if you don't stop what you are doing."

"Beth, your mouth just never stops going, does it? Now start working on your assignment."

Examples of positive teacher statements which would relate exclusively to the situation instead of to the student's character would be similar to the following:

"Ann, the coins are very distracting. Please put them in your pocket."

"Bob, see if you can't play with those children over there. I think they need another player."

"Beth, see if you can finish your assignment by the time we go out for recess."

A corollary to the principle of speaking to the situation and avoiding speaking to the character of the student is: SPEAK TO THE PRESENT, NOT TO THE PAST OR THE FUTURE.

A teacher speaking to the past: "Pat, you've done it again. I've told you a hundred times about that. What did I say yesterday?"

Or, "Last week it was one thing, yesterday another excuse. What now!"

"Paul, in your record here it shows you were sent home for fighting in the fourth grade. You were suspended for stealing in the fifth grade. And now you are working on cheating in the sixth grade. Looks like a fine record!"

Now, a teacher who speaks to the future: "Al, how are you ever going to hold a job after high school if you can't get to your eighth grade class on time."

"Chris, I can just imagine what kind of home you are going to keep when your desk looks like that."

"Jan, how are you going to make it through high school if you can't turn in these simple papers here."

Again, the appropriate thing to do is to speak to the present situation:

"Al, you are late. I lose time with class when I have to wait for you."

"Chris, let's get the desk cleaned out."

"Paul, cheating is inexcusable. Apparently, you want to do well but you must do your own learning."

"Jan, try to turn in your paper tomorrow. Perhaps you can start it now and I'll give you a hand."

SKILL #2: REDIRECTION

It is often best to avoid speaking to the problem at all. When a student is simply chatting or playing or out of seat when there is assigned work to do, the best thing may be to simply redirect the student toward the appropriate behavior. In other words, speak to the appropriate behavior, not the student's inappropriate behavior.

Example: A student is obviously writing notes to her friends instead of starting assigned work:

Wrong-- "Susan, perhaps you'd like to bring those notes to me."

Redirection-- "Susan, the assignment now is to read the story which begins on page 104. You'll be able to participate in our discussion later once you've read the story."

EXERCISE

For each of the following, write an expression (inappropriate) which speaks to the negative behavior of the student and then write one which serves to redirect the student by simply making him aware of the appropriate behavior for the moment.

1.   A boy is daydreaming in a second grade class when he has been given two worksheets to complete.

Wrong--

"
_____

_____
"

Redirection--

"
_____

_____
"

2.   A student who you know belongs in the library is standing at a classroom door looking in at other students.

Wrong--

"
_____

_____
"

Redirection--

"
_____

_____
"

3.   You have formed your class into groups of four students each to work out skits and you see one student at the window yelling out to others on the playground.

Wrong--

"_____

_____"

Redirection--

"_____

_____"

4. A student on the playground is poking with a stick at the corners of the school's basement windows instead of playing.
   Wrong--

   "_____

   _____"

   Redirection--

   "_____

   _____"

FEEDBACK

Redirection statements for each of those situations might be similar to the following:

1. "Pat, see if you can start on your first worksheet. Perhaps you can get both done by lunchtime. Let me know if you need help."

2. "Karen, you had better get to the library soon or else you'll need to go back to your classroom without having spent enough time in the library."

3.   "Dan, see if you can help your group."

4.   "Carey, why don't you see if you can join one of the students playing on the playground."

In each of the above situations, your redirecting response should mention only the appropriate behavior the student should be doing and should not mention or reflect anything about the inappropriate behavior the student is exhibiting.

SKILL #3:   "I-MESSAGES"

Psychologist Thomas Gordon (1974) advocates a type of communication which avoids telling the student what to do and avoids speaking to the student's character. Redirecting the student is appropriate for situations where a clear and specific assignment has been given or when the problem is minor, but telling students what to do (what you want them to do instead of what they want to do) often develops resentment. It often sounds very bossy, and causes the student to feel "pushed around."

"John, turn that radio down and put that magazine away."

"Pat, get off that window sill and sit down."

"Sandy, clean up that mess before you leave or you'll be working after school."

No one really likes to be bossed around, especially in front of their peers. Such demanding, directing statements often produce resentment (and frequently sarcastic "Yes, dear" responses).

Instead of telling the student what to do, with the "I-message" approach, you communicate the effect of the student's behavior on you.

Examples:

"John, the radio volume is making it difficult for me to work with students around the room. It is somewhat annoying."

50

"Pat, I get a little worried about someone sitting on the window sill and I get a little upset with a disorganized class."

"Sandy, I sure hope I don't have to clean up that mess. I don't think that would be fair."

Notice that in each example the student was <u>not</u> told what to do. Instead each student was told the effect of his or her behavior on the teacher. The more appropriate alternative student behavior was very clear, but left unsaid (implied). That way, the student can tell <u>himself</u> what to do. This may seem like a trivial difference, but it doesn't seem trivial to students. They are left with some autonomy to change their behavior on their own as opposed to having to do what they were told to do. This enables the student to do what seems correct without feeling like a pawn or a slave.

Notice in the "I-messages" that follow, that the teacher is communicating only the effect of the student's behavior on himself (or the class). There is no name calling, no bossing:

"Ron, it starts me off in a rather bad mood for class when you slam your books on your desk like that. It makes a rather unpleasant climate for all of us."

"Sara, when you throw paper in the room as I'm teaching, it tends to take my attention away from what I'm teaching, and I can't do my job."

"Bob, when you wear things that are not permitted, it really puts me in a bad position. I'm supposed to enforce the school rules and it sort of turns me into a tyrant."

EXERCISE

Write an "I-message" for each of the following situations to express the effect of the student's behavior on you.

51

Remember, do not tell the student what to do--leave that implied as you communicate <u>the</u> <u>effect</u> <u>of</u> <u>the</u> <u>student's</u> <u>behavior</u> <u>on</u> <u>you</u>.

1. Two students are chatting audibly as you try to teach a lesson to the whole class.

"_____

_____"

2. A student sticks gum under her desk.

"_____

_____"

3. A student borrows paper from you the fourth time in three days.

"_____

_____"

4. You hear a student use profanity more than once during small group discussions one day.

"_____

_____"

Check each of your reactions or "I-messages" to be sure that they have been written in such a way that . . .

1. They do not tell the student what to do; and
2. They do tell the effect of the student's behavior on you. Your "I-message" may communicate certain feelings the student's behavior produces in you, or it may communicate how it deprives you of certain rights, or it may indicate how the behavior prevents you from doing something you need to do. Note the following examples:

Feelings: "Sam, when I see you poking that turtle I get so angry I'd like to poke you. I really feel irritated, Sam."

Your Rights: "Carl, I believe I ought to be able to work all day in a reasonably clean room. When you dump all those paper clippings then I have to work all day in a mess."

Prevents Your Work: "Chris, I can't help these kids as I should when you are shouting like that."

FEEDBACK

Some examples of "I-messages" like those you may have written for the last exercise would be as follows:

1. "It's very difficult for me to maintain a good train of thought when I hear other people chatting in class."
2. "Sam, I often have to move desks around in here, and when I put my hands under the desks and feel gum there ... yuck. Also, someone has the unpleasant job of having to clean that off."
3. "I'm beginning to feel as though you are using me."
4. "Your profanity, Phil, bothers me a little being used in class like this."

WHAT IF THE "I-MESSAGE" DOESN'T WORK

Sometimes the student doesn't take the hint. He walks out without cleaning up the mess. She continues shouting. The implied message you sent is not received (or at least not acted upon). In this case, you have a problem. This calls for problem-solving.

Basically, this is a situation where you have a need (a clean room, a quiet work period, etc.) and the student has a need. Your need and the student's need conflict.

The usual adult response with children is to simply bring out the big guns and tell the students what to do, and in no uncertain terms. Of course, here again you have a situation ripe for hostility, resentment and revenge.

What would an adult do, however, with another adult? They would compromise ("Let's see how we can work this out so that both of us get what we need.").

When there is a conflict between your needs and a student's you can often try to find a way both of you can respect one another. When you have indicated how you want a clean room and a student continues tossing paper toward a wastebasket, you might communicate the following:

> "John, I really do need a reasonably clean room. Maybe you really need to entertain yourself when you've finished your assigned work. Perhaps I can have my clean room and you can read, write or draw instead of tossing paper."

When two students are chatting during a lesson, you might say:

> "I need to have everyone's attention when I'm explaining this. Perhaps you can jot notes to talk about with each other later."

In each case, the teacher avoided reprimand. Instead, she explained her needs (first through an "I-message") and

54

then, if necessary, thought of some compromise--some way both she and the student could get their way.

For each of the following, first write an "I-message" in response to the effect of the student's behavior on you. Then, assuming it has not been effective because the student's need is too strong to be eliminated with just an "I-message," develop a compromise. Write the compromise as you would actually verbalize it.

A. A boy is writing on his desktop.

"I-message":

"_____

_____"

Compromise:

"_____

_____"

B. A student is leaving his seat at every opportunity and you want to reduce this.

"I-message":

"_____

_____"

Compromise:

"_____

_____"

C. A student brings you some present nearly every day and you want to put an end to it.

55

"I-message":

"_____

_____"

Compromise:

"_____

_____"

SKILL #4: "OTHERS-MESSAGES"

Psychologist Martin Hoffman (in press) describes a skill similar to the use of Gordon's "I-message." Hoffman believes children can learn that their behavior has effects on others. Thus, when a student does something wrong, the teacher will point out the effects of the student's behavior on others. The teacher does not refer to punishment nor to character assassination.

Example: A student sticks gum under his desk.

Teacher ("others-message"): "Tom, other students have to sit there and most people don't enjoy a desk with gum stuck all over it. They may get it in their clothes. Also, the janitor will have to scrape that off."

A student pushes another who is at a drinking fountain.

Teacher ("others-message"): "Beth, it wouldn't feel good if Karen's mouth hits that fountain. If you stand in line, Karen can get a drink safely."

Notice that "others-messages" are appropriate only for problem behaviors which do affect another person.

EXERCISE

Place an I on any of the following which are examples of "I-messages" and place and O on any which are examples of "others-messages."

_____ 1. "Sam, leaving your bat there is likely to cause someone to trip and hurt themselves."

_____ 2. "Jim, whispering to Bob like that so often tends to get him into trouble more than he would like."

_____ 3. "Susan, I get awfully frightened when I see you spin the little kids around like that."

_____ 4. "When I hear a class laugh at someone like that I feel ashamed and embarrassed."

_____ 5. "Lou, it's difficult for the other teachers to enjoy the film when they have to be attending to you constantly."

Children who often hear of the effects of their behavior on others will no doubt become more and more aware that their behavior does affect others. Such an awareness is thought by some psychologists to have a relationship to the moral development of the child. We all know of people who seem to have no awareness and perhaps no concern that their behavior affects others (loud stereos in apartments, reckless driving).

EXERCISE

Write an "others-message" for each situation.

1. A girl is making marks on another girl's arm with her pen whenever the girl isn't looking.

    "Others-message"--

    "_____

    _____"

2. A student is running down the hall bumping into other students.

"Others-message"--

"   _____

_____   "

3. A young child is taking toys from another on the playground.

    "Others-message"--

    "   _____

    _____   "

4. A boy is helping another student cheat on a test.

    "Others-message"--

    "   _____

    _____   "

5. A student in Home Economics class is generally fooling around putting salt in someone's pie filling, splashing water with spoons, etc.

    "Others-message"--

    "   _____

    _____   "

So far, all the "others-messages" you have been writing are negative. That is, we have emphasized the negative effects of a student's behavior upon another.

It is also desirable to use <u>positive</u> "others-messages" when you see a student doing something that obviously has a very positive effect upon others.

Examples:

A child helps another pick up toys he was playing with. Teacher (positive "others-message"): "Tim, I can see Greg appreciates your help. He'll be done in no time."

A boy asks some others to quiet down during your lesson. Teacher (positive "others-message," after class): "Alan, it felt good to see you help me and the others have a smoother lesson today."

A student volunteers to be a "guide" for a new student in class.

Teacher (positive "others-message"): "Ginny, I imagine Terry appreciates your helping him learn his way around school like this. It must make him feel much more comfortable."

EXERCISE:

Write a positive "others-message" for each of the following situations:

1. A student volunteers an answer which others laugh at, but which one boy says out loud is "at least unique."

"_____

_____ "

2. A boy volunteers after school to walk home with another boy who has been very ill in school.

"_____

_____ "

3. A girl who usually talks a great deal during lessons is more quiet for a change.

"_____

_____."

SKILL #5: HUMOR

A teacher's sense of humor is generally an invaluable characteristic (Gnagey, 1981, p. 88). It can also be a valuable concrete skill when things go wrong, especially when the situation isn't terribly serious.

When a student sees that you are reacting to her misbehavior with a light sense of humor, she often feels much less resentment toward her teacher and more motivated to behave better. We are not speaking here of using jokes, nor even of trying to get laughs (certainly never at the student's expense). The skill is just to make light of the situation.

Examples:

To a boy who is out of his seat, as usual.

> "Kevin, I'm going to buy you roller skates one day. Just think how much more ground you'll be able to cover. Now please sit down and let me help you get started with your paper."

To a girl who throws paper airplanes in class:

> "Carol, I am sure the airlines will be after you. I wish I could get such smooth flights when I travel. Now, please begin your work on ..."

To a class when you come in and find cariacatures of yourself on the blackboard.

> "Oh, that's not me. Come on, now (draw funnier pictures). These teeth are much longer and the hair has to be standing up like that."

EXERCISE

Respond with humor or just light comments to the following situations.

1. A girl has her legs stuck out in the aisle.

"_____

_____"

2. A boy mimics another child.

"_____

_____"

3. A student is running to be first in line.

"_____

_____"

AN IMPORTANT NOTE: Much humor takes the form of disguised aggression. Sarcasm is such a form. There is no place in schools for humor which degrades the student--his behavior or character. Although a sarcastic bit of humor may seem funny to many in the class, the student against whom it is directed may very well be plotting his revenge.

SKILL SIX: STRAIGHT TALK

When you have noticed a student doing something wrong, especially if the student is trying to avoid being seen, it is often tempting to begin playing private detective.

Read the following example wherein a teacher has seen a boy sneak a piece of chalk into his pocket from the chalkboard and then whisper to his neighbor all the while as he should be working on his math problems. The teacher approaches the boy:

"Frank, what are you doing?"

"I'm...nothing."

"Oh, I think you're doing <u>something</u>. Can't you tell me what?"

"Fooling around?"

"My, my, you sure have a poor memory, Frank. Don't you have something that doesn't belong to you?"

"Uh...I don't know."

"Would you like to empty your pockets please?"

This dialogue may go on and on like this, the teacher probing as a detective giving the student several opportunities to confess and the student anxiously avoiding incriminating himself (do we expect him to say, "Oh yes, I just happened to have lifted a piece of chalk. Sorry?"). As the probing goes on and the student naturally avoids incriminating himself, the teacher adds to her rath because the child has not only stolen--he has also engaged in deceit!

The teacher has actually set up the situation for deceit. Now it may very well take some time for the resentment to subside.

What could the teacher have done instead? She could have clearly and simply let the student know what she saw (and redirect him). This is the skill we call <u>straight</u> <u>talk</u>:

"Frank, I saw you take chalk from the chalktray and put it in your pocket. Please put it back and begin your math work on page 23."

62

The teacher should not stand in front of the student and wait for him to obey. This more or less invites defiance and at least produces more a sense of resentment. Instead the teacher should walk away and check later to see if the chalk has been returned. This communicates to the student the idea that the teacher expects him to obey and trusts him to do it. A more general principle of human behavior is that we often tend to get what we expect. (A psychologist at a boy's detention home learned this the hard way. As he was leaving a boy's room at the end of a tense conversation, he noticed the boy holding a shoe. He felt the boy might be thinking of throwing the shoe at him. As he was leaving he looked over his shoulder cautiously and he got the shoe square in the head.) Thus when you ask a student to do something, it is generally better to act as if you have complete confidence that the student will obey. It won't always turn out that way but at least you won't be inviting defiance.

Now as you tackle the next exercise remember that the skill involved in straight talk means that you avoid probing and merely report what you have seen and what you expect the student to do. Remember, too, that it does very little good to ask a student why she or he has done something wrong. Often they don't know why.

EXERCISE

Now indicate in which of the following situations the teacher is responding with straight talk. Place an "S" beside straight talk statements and a "P" where the teacher is more of a private eye probing or giving the student a chance to confess.

_____ 1. A teacher senses a student has slipped gum into his mouth. "Bob, do you have anything in your mouth you shouldn't have, hmm?"

_____ 2. A teacher notices a girl looking onto another's paper during a test. "Kathy, please look at no one's paper but your own during a test."

_____ 3. A boy tells the playground supervisor that another has taken some of his lunch. The supervisor approaches the other boy. "Bill, do you have anything that doesn't belong to you?"

_____ 4. A teacher suspects an absence note was written by the student herself. "Jenny, was it your mother or father who wrote this note?"

_____ 5. A teacher sees that a student's desk is covered with fresh graffiti. "Pat, let me see all the pens you have in your desk. Why did you do this Pat?"

_____ 6. A principal notices a boy smoking outside the school and calls him in. "Ted, smoking is not permitted in the school nor on the grounds. Please observe that rule from now on."

FEEDBACK

In the situations above only the second and sixth responses were examples of straight talk. Now read the way a teacher who uses straight talk would respond to the other situations above (1, 3, 4 and 5):

1. "Bob, please get rid of what you put in your mouth and begin your art project now."

3. "Bill, give Jerry back what you took from him please."

4. "Jenny, it looks like your writing on this note. I hope you'll always have your mom and dad write you a note."

5. "Pat, please get some wet paper towels and clean off your desk."

Even the use of straight talk does not eliminate the possibility of getting into an argument. Bob might say he has nothing in his mouth. Bill might argue that he has taken nothing. If you can't possibly resolve the argument, it is better not to argue. If you're not going to make Bob open his mouth for an inspection then you might just tell him to begin his work. If, however, there are others who saw Bill take some of another boy's lunch you might confront him with that.

SKILL SEVEN: READ THE NEED

The communication skills for handling problem situations presented so far all have a common goal: they tend to reduce resentment in the student and to resolve the problem without making it worse.

The skill we present here goes even farther--it seeks to handle the problem and to help the student in a general way and to decrease further problems. When we "read the need" behind another's words, we are simply making a guess about what need motivates the person to say these things. Then our response is directed not at what the person said, but at the feelings and the needs behind the words. An example: A ten year old boy was placed in a foster home after being taken from his own abusive home by the court. At dinner time in his new home the following conversation took place.

Foster Mother: "Here Tom, have some meatloaf."

Tom: "Where I used to live we had steaks to eat."

Foster Mother (a little perturbed): "Well, you're not there now so you'll have to settle for meatloaf."

Tom: "My mother, she was a good cook. She never made no meatloaf."

Foster Mother: "If you don't like what we have, you can go without."

This woman might have realized that a boy from such a background who was now placed in a new and strange family might have very strong adjustment problems. This was a situation where reading the need would have helped. The mother might have asked herself, "Now what is he trying to tell us? Why does he say this?"

It doesn't take too much thought to realize the boy needs to think his original family was okay. It would even be natural for him to want to glorify his original family (abusive as they were) and to denigrate the people who are now putting themselves above his other family. Thus, we may want to reflect his need:

> "There were some pretty good things there which you had to leave... That was some family you had. Your mom...she was okay. It's tough to change families."

Notice that these comments do not refer to the content of the boy's remarks (steaks, good cook, etc.), but to the underlying message--the boy's need to affirm his background.

A little girl who was always dressed in very poor clothing was frequently overheard telling the other children that she had "lots of dresses at home. My mommy buys me clothes all the time, but I just save them for church." The girl's teacher responded inappropriately to the content of the girl's likely fibs:

> "Carrie, you don't have to say those things to us. We don't have to wear anything special to school. You look just fine."

The teacher might have asked himself: "What does this girl want from us. She wants us to think well of her, to think her family is okay, just as good as anyone's."

Reading the need the teacher might have said:

> "Well, your mother must really love you. I see every day that your hair is brushed and you're clean as a whistle. Your mom must surely be proud of you!"

66

The teacher avoided relating to the <u>content</u> of the girl's message but read the need conveyed by that message.

It is important to note that when you hear such "ego-enhancing" fibs and exaggerations that you need not always respond immediately. You may make a mental note that one child needs to feel accepted or that another needs to feel a sense of worthiness and later provide the appropriate evidence of such acceptance or worth.

EXERCISE

In the following examples indicate which teacher responses are reading the likely underlying need and avoiding the content of the student's message by placing a "N" on the response blank and indicate which are only relating to the <u>content</u> with a "C" on the blank.

1. A student new to a particular school says in various ways how things were so much better at his old school...the kids were smarter, the teachers weren't so bossy, "they had a real good gym."

____ Teacher 'A' response--"Leaving an old school is... well, it's pretty rotten isn't it. It's sort of like a family almost. You know, there's a little boy in the second grade who needs help learning to catch a ball. Do you think you could teach him for us?"

____ Teacher 'B' response--"John, I doubt the kids here are any less intelligent than at your old school and if the teachers are bossy... well, perhaps you can help by being friendlier."

2. A girl who brings her lunch in a paper sack when the other students all have fancy lunch boxes tells the others that she could have any lunch box she wanted but that she thought "lunch boxes were for babies."

____ Teacher 'A' response--"I guess everyone here is a baby then...is that right Trish?"

____ Teacher 'B' response (to himself)--"Trish feels defensive and perhaps bitter that she couldn't have a lunch box. At least she feels 'out of it'. I'll have to be sure to give her some special attention later."

3. A boy is boasting to others who are taunting him that he has a big brother who will beat them up. The teacher knows, however, that he has no brothers.

____ Teacher 'A' response--"You'd like to take care of those guys wouldn't you. They pick on you and it makes you feel like bringing out the Army."

____ Teacher 'B' response--"Tom, I didn't realize that you had brothers!"

4. A girl whose parents didn't come to school to see her in a class play tells her teacher that her parents were sick.

____ Teacher 'A' response-"I hope your parents are better soon, Sue. Do they have flu like everyone else these days?"

____ Teacher 'B' response-"I'm sorry I didn't get to meet them, Sue."

Now write a response indicating that you can read the need underlying the two situations presented below. Respond to the need, not the content.

1. A high school girl who has no date for a dance tells everyone she could have had lots of dates. Now she seems upset as she tells about the boys she turned down.

Now, write a response indicating that you can read the need of this child to have you feel that she isn't undesirable.

_____

_____

2. A girl playing with toys other children brought to
   school boasts that she has "much nicer toys than
   these."

_____

_____

Unit References

Faust, N. Discipline and the classroom teacher. Port
   Washington, NY: Kennikat Press, 1977.

Ginott, H. Teacher and child. New York: Avon, 1972.

Gnagey, W. J. Motivating classroom discipline. New York:
   Macmillan Publishing Co., 1981.

Gordon, T. Teacher effectiveness training. New York: David
   McKay Co., 1974.

Hoffman, M. L. Moral development. In M. Lamb and
   M. Bornstein (Eds.) Developmental psychology: An
   advanced textbook. Hillsdale, NJ: Lawrence Erlbaum
   Associates Inc., (in press).

Howell, R. G. and Howell, P. L. Discipline in the classroom:
   Solving the teaching puzzle. Reston, VA: Reston Publishing Co., 1979.

Lepper, M. R. Social control processes, attributions of motiva-
tion, and the internalization of social values. In
E. T. Higgins, D. N. Ruble, and W. W. Hartup (Eds.),
Social cognition and social behavior: Developmental
perspectives. Cambridge, England: Cambridge University
Press, 1983.

Walker, H. M. The acting-out child: Coping with classroom
disruption. Boston: Allyn and Bacon, 1979.

UNIT FIVE
SOME SPECIAL PROBLEMS

I. Cheating

Cheating behavior arouses particular anger in teachers. Cheating is a form of deception, and being deceived is akin to being made a fool.

But why do we cheat? Is cheating a character trait in some children? A great deal of research tells us that almost everyone cheats at some time and that cheating in one situation does not necessarily predict cheating in another. What does seem to underlie cheating is expediency--the degree of effort required and the risk of detection. In other words, cheating is likely if it is easy to do and if it is easy to get away with.

Of course, other factors seem related to cheating: the stake, or how important the outcome is (a message was recently observed on a T-shirt--"Anything worth having is worth cheating for"); the student's self-confidence may also determine whether she needs to cheat.

Now, imagine you are giving your students a test and you notice that one student is obviously glancing at a small piece of paper poorly hidden on his seat. What do you do? What will you say?

If your own self-confidence or sense of worthiness is shaky, you may feel you are being made a fool. Your un-spoken reaction may be, "I'll show him!" You may feel the student is "trying to get away with something, trying to 'take advantage'."

In this case you walk with vengence toward the student and say with venom on your tongue, "Give me that paper." You tear it up, walk to your desk and record an 'F' in your gradebook.

But if you do not have such a poor self-concept yourself and if you feel instead very sure of yourself and professional in your work with students, your personal reaction may be, "Now there's Ken cheating. I wish I could do something to help that kid." You approach the student calmly and say privately and quietly, "Ken, I see you looking on another paper here (straight talk). You must want to do well on this test. I guess you don't feel confident about it. Since I haven't seen you cheat before, I'll let you come in tomorrow and retake the test. I really want you to learn this, Ken, but I'll have to reduce your grade a little in fairness to the others who don't have extra time."

You have shown here that you are not "out to get" anyone. Your reaction has been an understanding statement reflecting the student's likely feelings. Are you, however, inadvertently reinforcing cheating behavior by being so understanding? That is a reasonable question, but the answer is not so certain. How would _you_ feel if you were that student? Would the teacher's response make you feel more like cheating, or would it make you feel a bit more ashamed of having cheated. There is no evidence that students will cheat more often when the teacher takes a more understanding approach and it is very likely that such an approach will actually give the student more reason to be honest in the future. If your responses are consistently nonvindictive and more professional, the student is more likely to see you as a teacher (perhaps his _only_ teacher) who really cares about him.

Now it may be that this student has cheated before. It is not quite so easy to be understanding this time, yet a vindictive response still does no good and likely will lead to poorer rapport. This time you can still provide a professional response showing concern for the student even if you do not allow him a makeup opportunity.

"Ken, I see you still have a need to bring your answers to the test in writing. I wish I could help you learn better so you wouldn't have to do this. I can't give you any credit for learning when you apparently can't do it without that aid. Why don't you stop by after school and I'll see if we can't find some solution to this problem."

EXERCISE

Now imagine that you have assigned a short story to be written by your students. While reading them you come across one that you know is straight out of a teen magazine (because you are familiar with these magazines). You call the student to your desk at the end of class. Write a professional statement you can make to the student that involves straight talk (avoid probing detective work) and a reflection of the student's probable feelings and needs leading to the plagiarism.

"

_____

_____

_____

"

_____

Now write the same sort of response you would make to two students who have turned in identically wrong and right answers on a take-home test.

"

_____

_____

_____

"

_____

II. Lying

Have you ever lied to anyone? Why did you lie? Were you afraid the truth would make you look foolish or stupid or would embarrass you? Perhaps you were afraid the truth would hurt the other person. It may have been, too, that you would have received punishment or penalty for telling the truth. These are the reasons most people lie, but when children lie to us, we feel particular anger and vengeance. Again, this is probably due to the way we let ourselves feel "taken advantage of" when deceived. A professional response, however, is not an emotionally vindictive response.

Imagine a teacher sees a student chewing gum and asks her to put it in the wastebasket. Shortly he asks the student if she has done it and the girl says she did. Later the girl forgets her lie and cracks her gum as she talks with friends in class. The teacher sees and hears the act and calls the girl to his desk. In this case the teacher is understandably angry and decides to use an I-message.

"Jane, I _really_ get angry when you lie to me. I feel like...getting even."

Then he attempts to put himself in the student's place and provide a bit of understanding: He says calmly,

"Perhaps you really disagree with the rule about chewing gum. I guess you must. Maybe you feel by defying me on this you can feel a little less pushed around. You don't normally lie to me. I hope you don't feel we're in a contest to score points against each other. We do have some rules."

EXERCISE

Read the following situations and indicate with the letters _Pro_ which of the two responses is the more professional.

1. A girl writes on her desk, scratching the surface, and the teacher tells her that she need not stay after school as punishment if she tells her parents about the situation and brings a note from them. She

74

brings the note the following day and says she told her parents. The teacher calls the home to confirm the situation and finds that the girl did not tell the parents and wrote her own note.

_____ Teacher A response:

> "Theresa, I talked to your parents and was told you did not tell them about the problem. They know now, of course. I guess you couldn't bring yourself to tell them something like that. It was too awkward perhaps."

_____ Teacher B response:

> "I understand you did not tell your parents of this problem, Theresa, but you stood right there and told me you did, didn't you. You told me you would tell them and then you didn't. Is this the way you're going to get out of problems the rest of your life?"

2. A student who sees the counselor regularly attempting to overcome discipline problems gets into a serious fight. When the counselor asks about his progress he says he hasn't gotten into any problems. The counselor, of course, learns about the fight from the principal. Later the counselor sees the student again.

_____ Counselor A response:

> "Dave, I thought you told me last time you haven't been in any problems. You tell me that--then I hear a half hour later that you have been in serious problems. Do you need to add lying to your problems?"

_____ Counselor B response:

"I understand you had been in a pretty serious fight before our last session. I guess you were a little embarrassed to tell me. You know, I don't expect you do be super human, Dave. I do hope you'll be able to cut down on these problems though."

3. A librarian asks a teacher to remind one of her students about a book which is overdue. The teacher tells the librarian that the student has been using it in class to work on an overdue report. The librarian sees the boy later and asks him to bring the book in. The boy says he lost it at home and that his mother is looking for it.

_____ Librarian A response:

"Greg, your teacher told me you have that book in class. I guess you must really need it badly to make up a story like that. Another student needs the book, Greg, so please return it."

_____ Librarian B response:

"Greg, your teacher just told me that you have that book in class. Your sense of honesty isn't any better than your sense of responsibility!"

Now write a professional response to each of the following situations, reflecting at least some degree of understanding instead of harsh and defensive or sarcastic remarks.

1. A student tells his teacher he wants to go to the library. When the teacher checks on him she finds he hasn't gone there but has gone to his sister's classroom instead.

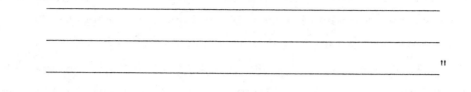

"

_____

_____

_____ "

2. A teacher finds that a student <u>has</u> taken a book from another student after the student told the teacher he hadn't taken the book.

" _____

_____

_____ "

3. A teacher asks all students in a photo club to work at their photo fair, but one girl says that she has to work that evening. The teacher stops at a drug store and encounters the girl with her new boyfriend.

" _____

_____

_____ "

III. Profanity

Profanity seems particularly inappropriate to most people and particularly in certain situations: informal public situations (a business meeting, etc.) when used excessively, when used toward superiors or even in the presence of superiors, or in the presence of certain people in authority, and when used by children. Those last two conditions and the first cover profanity used in schools. Consequently, a teacher's reaction is likely to be rather intense. In fact, it is not uncommon for a student to be suspended from school for using profanity as a means of expression.

In order to form an understanding of a professional response to such an expression, it is helpful to consider the likely reasons a student would swear in school.

Do you ever swear? Do you ever feel like swearing in a public or formal situation or when in the presence of an authority? Why? Could it be anger or frustration or disgust combined with perhaps habit? Does it just slip out at times? Are you more likely to use profanity if others around you are using it? All these reasons probably relate to the use of profanity by students in schools.

Other reasons also influence children in such situations. Children often want to impress others with their "maturity." Using profanity, like smoking, is a child's way of feeling grown up. It is also a way of imitating peers or older brothers or parents. One teacher told the story of how a child's parents had to be called to the school for a conference because the child was using such obscene language. The child's mother came in, sat down and began:

"What the *#!?*# has the *#!?*# kid been doing now? I've been called to this *#!?*# school three times this year." The teacher gained perfect insight into why that child was using obscenities.

Incidentally, while young children usually sense that obscenities are "bad" words (which seldom fail to upset adults) they often have no idea of the actual meaning of the words. For example, a ten-year-old girl was imploring her seven-year-old brother to accompany her trick-or-treating at Halloween. Her concern was protection.

"Oh," he said, "you want me to protect you from the hookers?"

His sister looked perplexed.

"What do you mean?" she asked.

"You know," he replied. "Hookers, teenagers who go around beating kids up, you know, with the 'old left hook'!"

A professional response to the student's use of profanity recognizes that the underlying need is often attention-getting or a need to impress others with one's worldliness. Thus a professional response to such language is one which reads the need. Examples:

A teacher often hears a young man muttering obscenities. He approaches the boy privately and says:

"Joe, it's very unusual for students to be using profanity in classes. If you want my attention I guess you got it."

Another teacher overhears a student complaining about another teacher. She hears the student refer to the teacher with an unkind, obscene word. The teacher approaches the girl and says:

"Carol, you sound pretty angry. I don't usually hear you or other students use profane language in school. Your feelings must really be...well, you must be awfully upset."

You can see that the teacher is attempting to understand the student's underlying needs. In the first example the need was attention. In the second example the need was expression of anger or resentment. In each case the teacher did not tell the student to stop nor did the teacher reprimand the student, nor make the student feel dirty-minded. Yet the student is probably even more likely to stop since the teacher has shown a degree of understanding. If the teacher had said something sarcastic or demeaning or threatening to the student a common pattern might have developed:

The student would mutter another obscenity under his or her breath as the teacher walked away. Then the teacher turns on her heel and says:

"WHAT DID YOU SAY?"

The student replies:

"Nothing."

Then the teacher threatens again and a power struggle ensues.

EXERCISE

For each of the following situations write a response which reflects an understanding of the student's underlying need and which avoids condemning the student (it is certainly appropriate to suggest if you wish that the student use more acceptable language while in school and it may be often perfectly accept able to simply ignore what you have heard if the occurrence is fairly rare).

1. A student has a difficult time closing his desk top and swears in the process. You happen to overhear his expression.

"
_____

_____

_____"

2. A girl is being teased by a boy near her and she calls him a rather obscene name.

"
_____

_____

_____"

3. You come into your classroom and notice a student darting away from the blackboard having written some mild obscenities there.

"
_____

_____

_____ "

IV. Substandard Language

Pictured on the cover of one of the National Education Association's magazines was a group of boys playing football. One boy was pictured as saying, "Who bungled that play?" Another confessed, "It was I." This was intended, of course, to show how ridiculous it would be for a child to use perfect grammar in such a situation.

Almost no one speaks English in a purely grammatical form at all times. Some might argue that a boy who responded as the example above would have a difficult time for himself. Yet in classrooms we do expect students to use at least something like standard English most of the time. Children, like adults, do not like to have their language corrected and generally react with apathy when criticized.

A student may say, "I gots one of those at home." The teacher may correct the student: "We don't say gots, Peter. You should say 'I have one of those at home'." The student's reply: "Whatever." The alternatives to directly and publicly correcting substandard language are fairly simple and straightforward:

1. Respond to the student with a phrase similar to his own, using standard English.
2. Make a written note of the error you hear and include it later in a language lesson.

Responding to the student may be illustrated as follows:

1. Student: "I gots one of those at home."

   Teacher: "You have one at home, Pete?" (Note that the reply is a question, not an attempt to correct grammar. There is no emphasis on the word "have".

2. Teacher: "Where's Tommy?"

   Student: "He's went already."

   Teacher: "He went already? Good."

3. Student: "I ain't got none now."

   Teacher: "You don't have any?"

EXERCISE

Now write a response in standard English for each of the following:

1. "I don't have no pencils of his."

   "_____

   _____"

2. "He shouldn't oughta done that."

   "_____

   _____"

3. "We has the best team, man."

   "_____

   _____"

REMEMBER--A teacher hearing the first two expressions would also make a note to conduct a lesson on the error of double negatives.

V. Tattletales

One of the most common and most quickly irritating behaviors in elementary schools is one student reporting on another. Although this behavior seems to reach a peak around the second grade and third grade levels, it extends even through junior high school and high school levels.

Hearing students telling on one another every other minute is singularly exasperating. Consequently, a teacher's response is often considerably less than professional. To determine an appropriate form of response to such behavior it is valuable to first consider what we want to happen because of our response.

Do you want the child to stop telling on others completely? If so, then we would respond with anger and perhaps threat: "Oh, honestly Jane, if you tell on someone one more time I'm going to sit you in the corner."

Yet, most teachers do want children to feel some degree of social responsibility. We don't want to encourage children to close their eyes to wrongdoing. Nor do we want to give them the idea that we are not concerned about such behavior. A second possibility then is that you would want the children to report to you so you could handle the problem: "Thank you, Jane. I'll look into it in a minute." In this case, however, we know intuitively that we are probably encouraging the student to use us as weapons in all their little conflicts. Furthermore, we run the risk of wearing ourselves out playing police officer.

Fortunately there are alternative responses to tattletales which do not have such undesirable side effects. One form of response is to first practice reflective listening and then to ask the student what they think they might do about the problem.

Example: An eight-year-old boy runs to his teacher and says another boy won't let him play with a certain toy. The teacher responds:

> "You'd like that toy and he's playing with it and won't give it up. Is that the problem?"
> "Yes," the boy replies. "He's had it more than me."
> "You're mad because it doesn't seem fair to you. What would be good for you to do now?"

After reflecting what is heard of the boy's problem and his <u>feeling</u> about it, the teacher asked him to consider a plan. The teacher should stay with the boy and repeat if necessary that the boy should consider what the right thing would be to do.

Note that the teacher did not scold the child, did not call the child tattletale, did not ask the child, "Well, what did <u>you</u> do?" The teacher reflected the student's concern (thus conveying some respect) and asked him to take responsibility for his conflicts (also a form of respect).

EXERCISE

Develop a response to each of the following situations which reflects the student's concern and encourages the student to handle the problem himself or herself:

1. A student runs up to you on the playground and complains that the girls won't get off the baseball area.

"
_____

_____
                                              "
_____

2. A student comes to you and reports that another student is chewing gum.

"
_____

_____

_____ "

3. A student reports to you about another student not returning a borrowed pencil.

"
_____

_____

_____ "

If you use such responses regularly, students are likely to learn quickly that they cannot count on you to intervene as a heavy-handed problem solver every time something goes wrong.

Another approach used successfully by many teachers is to ask the students to write their complaints. This is especially effective if a student has a serious grievance with another. The teacher may ask the alleged offending student to write a version of the story as well. The teacher may ask each student to place his or her report on the teacher's desk, then the teacher holds a conference at a later, more appropriate time reporting to both students about how each feels and asking them to work out a solution. Perhaps more often than not the student telling on another will not want to bother with writing an official complaint and will go about his or her business solving the problem eventually. Yet the teacher has shown concern and offered opportunity for action if the situation were serious enough.

RIDICULERS

Some of any student's darkest days in school are made that way by other students. Students will make fun of others for the slightest of reasons and will often continue the harassment until the poor victim either retaliates or withdraws into a shell. One of the most common teacher responses to such behavior is--no response. The teacher often ignores such behaviors.

One problem with developing a professional response to this behavior is that we fear any response will further embarrass the victim. Unfortunately, to overlook such ridiculing is to aid the aggressor and to increase the other child's suffering.

Making fun of others is a very deeply ingrained childhood behavior and consequently not easy to eradicate. Perhaps more than any other problem behavior, ridiculing requires a consistent, systematic approach.

One method for controlling this problem is to wait until about two weeks into the school year and then indicate to your class what you have been hearing. You might say that you've often heard someone making fun of another's clothing or that you have heard someone ridiculing another's choice of words.

Then you can hold a well planned guidance lesson on the reasons we ridicule others. Students should be encouraged to suggest answers, but the teacher should be certain to make students aware of the following reasons we might ridicule others.

1. The other person reminds us of what we are afraid of being.
2. Ridiculing is a way of developing group guidelines (norms) for behavior so that everyone can know that he is okay just by following these guidelines.
3. We have the irrational idea or belief that everyone should be just like ourselves.

86

4. We might ridicule another to make ourselves look better.

Can you think of other reasons?

_____

_____

_____

The teacher can lead a discussion beforehand on the concept of ridiculing. The students may have their own language for this behavior and use expressions such as: digs, putdowns, etc. But everyone knows what it means to be made fun of.

Then, the teacher can lead a discussion that clarifies the reasons presented above and those suggested by students. Plenty of illustrations are helpful. The teacher might explain that a boy who was once very frail may make fun of others for what he dislikes about himself (his past). Students might be asked if there should be official, explicit guidelines which would require particular clothing, particular haircuts, particular word usage, etc. Would students like to have uniforms? The alternative, of course, is to value diversions and individual expression and the teacher may ask the class to make an official commitment to such a value.

Later when the teacher hears a putdown he can simply allude to the commitment. After the class agrees, as they might, that they should give up the idea that everyone should be just like them (and recognize the impossibility of that), then the teacher hearing a putdown can also allude to the student's irrational belief. When the students indicate they understand (through examples and discussion) how we make ourselves look better by putting down others, then the teacher can also allude to someone's "cheap gain" when hearing such ridicule.

An effective way to teach this notion is to illustrate how one's "ego-gain" from putting down others is analogous to the motion of a teeter totter. The teacher illustrates on the blackboard how we put ourselves up on the teeter totter by putting the other person down. Then with several examples and some planned role playing the teacher shows how one student can put himself up (make himself _seem_ superior) by "putting another down." Later when the teacher hears a "putdown" he can look at the offender and use some expression such as "someone's going down, someone must be going up." It might also be helpful to ask students to observe this behavior in their friends and schoolmates and to hold a discussion later to follow up on their observations.

In conclusion, we have indicated that a teacher can hold well-planned discussions on the problem of ridiculing and the reasons we often ridicule others. Then when "putdowns" are heard the teacher can respond by alluding to:

1. a _commitment_ the class has made to respecting individuality and differences.

2. the offender's apparent belief that everyone should be like him or her.

3. the ego gain one is getting by putting another down.

Example:

1. After holding a rather involved discussion on individual differences and the concept of putdowns, a teacher hears a student make fun of another student's library book choice.

> Teacher's Response: "Jack, apparently you believe that _everyone_ should check out the kind of book _you_ like. Remember, we made a commitment to respect individual choices."

88

2. Later the same teacher hears a student take a jab at another student's poor athletic ability.

> "John, do you feel in a superior position now that you have put someone beneath you? We made a commitment, John, to improve ourselves <u>without</u> hurting others."

EXERCISE

For the following three situations, develop a response based upon the reasons explained above for ridiculing and the commitment your students might have made.

1. You hear a student make fun of another's poor reading ability.

"_____

_____

_____"

2. You hear a student make fun of another for trying so hard to be a good student.

"_____

_____"

3. You hear a student put down another because of a mistake in pronouncing a word.

"_____

_____

_____"

AN IMPORTANT NOTE:

It is obvious in these situations that the teacher is responding to negative behavior. Often the best response is to ignore a behavior in order to avoid increasing that behavior because of the attention you pay it. Consequently, if ridiculing is a very low frequency behavior in your classroom, you may want to ignore it or simply redirect the offender to the task at hand. In many public school classrooms, however, ridiculing is such a high frequency behavior that ignoring it will not make it go away. Consequently, the teacher must respond with a professional approach as suggested above.

When you notice that the frequency reduces, you might recognize that verbally. Tell the students in such a case that you feel they have developed considerable maturity and that it feels good to teach in a classroom where people respect each other.

It is often quite effective in such circumstances to begin emphasizing behaviors which seem quite opposite to the problem behaviors. The behavior which would seem quite opposite to the attitude behind ridiculing would be respect for individual differences. A teacher might ask students to develop posters, to develop skits, or to create short stories on the theme of respect for individual differences. Students who are concentrating on ways in which they can show a value for respecting individual differences and human variance will find it difficult to be ridiculing others simply because they are different.

UNIT SIX
PREVENTING PROBLEMS

Professional and effective communication patterns are helpful not only in handling problem situations such as lying, cheating, swearing, etc., but they can also keep many problems from otherwise arising.

SAVING FACE

When a teacher needs to direct a reprimand to a single student, it is best done privately. Otherwise, unforeseen problems may arise.

Example:

One teacher began the new school year with an eighth grade boy he had also had as a seventh grade student. This student was somewhat troublesome and viewed himself as a power figure among the junior high students. Having given the class an assignment to begin, the teacher noticed this boy was not beginning to work but was beginning to look around for fun. The teacher spoke loudly and firmly from his desk, "Tom, get to work."

The student replied: "You shut up or I'll come up there and smack you upside the head."

This exchange of course led to considerable trouble and the student was transferred to another class.

But why would a student behave in such a threatening way? A part of the problem was his apparent need for face-saving. This boy was one of the biggest, toughest, roughest kids in school. The teacher had just publicly "bossed" him as all students were listening. In order to maintain his own image of his place among his peers, he had to show everyone that he could not be pushed around--he had to save face. A part of his problem was his apparent need to save his reputation (not having to hide your face in public).

91

Now, if the teacher had walked up to the student's desk, he could have quietly repeated the assignment to the boy (re-direction) and the boy's reaction would likely have been totally different. Because no one else would have heard the inter-action, there would have been no need to save face among peers.

Example:

A junior high teacher on playground duty noticed a girl bouncing a rubber ball against the school building, a behavior strictly forbidden. The teacher approached the girl and told her to stop bouncing the ball against the building.

The student looked at her, said, "Okay," then bounced the ball deliberately one more time against the wall. The student's reaction completely unnerved the teacher and the student ended up sitting on the steps for the rest of the lunch break as punishment.

The problem here was a form of the need for face-saving. The student was doing something she wanted to be doing and someone told her to stop the behavior which was repetitiously in motion (when we are making some motion such as tapping a pen over and over, the repetitiveness seems to create each motion as a stimulus for the next, a sort of limited perpetual motion).

Even though there was no audience of peers in this situ-ation, the girl was still engaging in face saving as a reaction to having her behavior sequence controlled by someone else's command. No one likes to feel like a pawn, and the point here is that we can expect such face saving when we attempt to control a student's behavior as in this example. The alterna-tive in this situation might be simply to call the student away from the wall and explain the effects of her behavior on others inside the building ("others-message") and suggest another place to bounce the ball.

EXERCISE

Place an <u>F</u> on the blank beside each situation in which the student would likely feel the need for <u>face-saving</u>:

_____A. A teacher sees a boy standing near a hall bulletin board unconsciously peeling off bits of paper from the edges as he talks with another student. The teacher approaches the boy and says, "Pete, Mr. Andrews put a lot of work into that bulletin board."

_____B. A teacher sees a student tossing pebbles at a school bus tire as all the students are gathering to board the bus. The teacher yells for the boy to stop it.

_____C. A group of students is gathered for rehearsal on the school auditorium stage and one girl seems to be showing off. A teacher yells at her saying, "Janice, we don't need hams until tomorrow night."

_____D. A student in a science class is seen to be looking at his partner's workbook constantly. The teacher approaches the student and says, "Kim, you seem to need a lot of help with your workbook. Will you come to me when you need help."

COMMUNICATING EXPECTATIONS

One cause of many problems in school is the teacher's failure to clearly communicate expectations. It is often amazing how just telling someone what we expect increases the likelihood of their doing it! Expecting something of another person without communicating that expectation is often simply a way of setting yourself up for problems:

-- A girl would like her boyfriend to be less affectionate in public. She never tells him what she wants in this regard and the problem boils within her.

-- A mother would like her daughter to speak cordially to her guests as the daughter passes through the house but never bothers to tell her daughter what she'd like.

93

<u>Communicating Rules and Procedures</u>. Most experts on school discipline agree that it is helpful to have some <u>positively</u> <u>stated</u> rules spelled out for your classes (Weber, 1982). These rules may be discussed with the students and may in some cases be posted in the classroom. Stating rules positively conveys your expectations for positive behavior:

Example:

    Negative: No running in the classroom.

    Positive: Walk in classroom and halls. Running permitted on playground.

    Negative: No gum chewing.

    Positive: Eat and chew gum in the <u>cafeteria</u>.

    Negative: No shouting, yelling, etc.

    Positive: Quiet talking please.

Consequently a teacher who is concerned about the problems above may have a poster in his or her classroom with the following rules:

    A. Walk in classroom and halls. Running permitted on playground.

    B. Eat, and chew gum in cafeteria.

    C. Quiet talking please.

EXERCISE

    Write on the blanks below at least three more rules a teacher or school might communicate in positive terms.

_____

_____

_____

<u>Rehearsal</u>. One way of clearly conveying your expectations to students is to: 1) tell them clearly how to proceed; then, 2) have the students rehearse the behavior in the way you requested.

Example:

A teacher who realized how unrestrained youngsters can be at dismissal time told her students that she expected them each day to <u>walk</u> out of the class quietly and to <u>walk</u> down the stairs patiently and quietly. Then she asked students to explain what walking downstairs patiently would mean. Then, as it was the end of the school day, she gave the students a chance to practice. She positioned herself on the landing of the stairs and rewarded the students the next day with extra recess time because they had done exactly as she asked. Thereafter she remembered to occasionally remind the students of the procedure just before dismissal.

The teacher followed four steps:

1. She clearly told the students the behaviors she expected.

2. She had the students rehearse the behavior as she observed.

3. She rewarded the students.

4. She remembered to remind them (to <u>cue</u> them) now and then just before they would perform the behavior.

EXERCISE

Now incorporate these four steps into an example of your own about a teacher attempting to start students off correctly on some behavior (such as going to gymnasium, eating in cafeteria, etc.).

_____

_____

_____

_____

_____

_____

_____

_____

Communicating Clearly. One of the most overused words in schools may be the word attitude:

"Bonnie has a poor attitude."

"You'd better change that attitude young man."

"An attitude like that will get you into trouble."

Just what does the teacher want from each student in these expressions? It may be as difficult for the student to tell as for us. Communicating clearly in order to communicate expectations requires that we refer to specific behavior:

The teacher indicating a student has a poor attitude may mean:

- he sleeps in class

- he rests his head in his hand

- he doesn't smile at the teacher

- he fails to hand in homework

or,

the teacher may mean:

- he criticizes the teacher's opinions

- he seems closed-minded on certain subjects

- he seems to dislike the teacher

Whatever the teacher means, she would do better to refer to specific behaviors rather than to general, unclear notions.

A teacher may often say something such as, "Now you kids are going to have to shape-up and start behaving yourselves." Do the students know exactly what to do because this teacher asked them to shape-up?

He might have meant that they should be quiet when they enter his classroom, or he might have meant that they should get their materials out immediately. At any rate, the students may not be sure of exactly what he meant. Of course, the teacher knows what he meant, but the students won't know until he tells them specifically.

EXERCISE

Indicate on the blanks below each situation how a teacher might communicate specific behaviors as expectations instead of the vague expectations indicated:

Vague

A.   "I want you to behave yourself in the library today."
Specific

"_____   _____

_____

_____"

Vague

B.   "I want you people to show some enthusiasm on that stage."
Specific

"_____

_____

_____"

Vague

C.   "I want you all to act like ladies and gentlemen when we go to this movie."

Specific

"

_____

_____

_____ "

The Five Minute Warning.   Many parents and teachers have
learned that unpleasant problems can often be prevented by
giving children a warning signal a few minutes before they are
expected to stop playing or watching television, etc.   Psychologists have termed this technique a form of cueing (Gnagey,
1981).

When students become engrossed in some activity, it is
difficult for them to switch to something else without warning.
Telling youngsters that they have five more minutes to finish
what they are doing allows them to psychologically withdraw at
their own pace.

The five minute warning might be used in such situations
as:

- when students are doing artwork: "Okay, five minutes before cleanup."
- when students are playing a game in a gym.   "Five
minutes before showers."
- when students are working in groups: "Only five
more minutes now before we all get back together."

EXERCISE

Indicate two situations in which you could express a five
minute warning similar to those above.

" _____ "

" _____ "

Communicating Expectations Nonverbally

Does a person's nonverbal behavior communicate anything about expectations? Read again the following true account we alluded to in an earlier section:

> A young psychologist working in a juvenile detention center was talking with a teenage boy in the boy's room. The boy was angry and bitter and the discussion took an unfortunate turn toward conflict. The psychologist thought he should leave as he saw the boy clutching a heavy shoe with vengence in his eyes. As the psychologist was leaving the room fear motivated him to glance over his shoulder to see if the boy might be planning to throw the shoe. Sure enough, the boy hurled the shoe then directly at the psychologist's head.

The psychologist knew later that by looking back over his shoulder he had communicated the expectation that the boy would throw the shoe!

Another happier example comes from a psychiatrist who also worked in the juvenile detention center. This psychiatrist was called to a section of the building where a young man was terrorizing everyone in sight by wielding a large chair over his head. The psychiatrist came to the area and approached the boy. "Look," he said. "I haven't had dinner yet and I was just on my way home. Apparently you want attention from one of us so I'll come right back after I eat. Sit down for awhile and wait." Then he turned and walked away without hesitating and without glancing back. The boy put the chair down and the psychiatrist came back in fifteen minutes and everything ended happily.

In this case the psychiatrist communicated his expectation that the boy would do as he requested. He gave him a reason (he had to eat), and his behavior showed that he didn't doubt for a moment that the boy would do as asked. Now obviously this won't work every time, but it is a general principle worth practicing.

99

Example:

A teacher sees a girl sitting on a delicate display table: "Chris, will you please find a seat now." The teacher then walks on about other business without standing in front of the girl and without watching for her to leave. Later if she sees the girl has not obeyed she may use a strong I-message: "Chris, I worry when I see a student on that table...and it disappoints me to see that you need to be asked twice."

EXERCISE

Place a check on the blank beside each situation in which a teacher is <u>indirectly</u> communicating the expectation that the student will do as asked:

_____ 1. A teacher sees a student loitering near a drinking fountain obviously out of class. The teacher tells the student to return to class and walks on past the student to the school office.

_____ 2. A teacher who has to leave her classroom momentarily sternly warns the students to behave themselves, leaves the room and turns back immediately to check on them.

_____ 3. A drama teacher has a number of students rehearsing a play and tells them that she has to leave for a few minutes and knows that they will rehearse their parts as though she were there.

_____ 4. A teacher on playground notices that a student has torn a paper bag into many small pieces and left them lay on the ground. He approaches and tells the boy to pick up every piece and stands watching until every piece is picked up.

_____ 5. A teacher giving a test seats each student at a particular desk with one seat vacant between each person.

Additionally, the teacher has placed code numbers on each test and indicates that alternative forms of the test have been distributed.

In the situations described above only the first and third illustrate a teacher indirectly communicating that he or she trusts the student will behave as requested or expected.

The teachers in the second, fourth and fifth situations all communicate a sense of mistrust. Their actions say, "I expect you won't do as I have asked unless I threaten you, watch you, keep an eye on you." In the last example it wouldn't be unusual for some students to feel a significant challenge and to attempt to subvert the teacher's elaborate attempts to create honesty where the teacher obviously expects dishonesty.

The point here, of course, is that our indirect and non-verbal behavior conveys expectations which are frequently fulfilled by the students. One kindergarten teacher proved this point to herself. With one class she brought a number of new, attractive toys into the classroom and put them on a table. Then she turned to the students and said threateningly, "These toys are for later. Don't touch them. Anyone who touches these is going to be sorry. Now I have to leave the room for ten minutes. Behave yourselves." While the teacher was away a videotape camera recorded activity around the table.

To another class she brought the same toys. Again she set them on the table and said, "These toys are for later. Can you please decide for yourself to leave these for later today?" Then she again announced that she had to leave for ten minutes and again the camera recorded any transgressions.

In which class do you think more students touched the toys? Intuitively you may imagine that the teacher communicated indirectly to the first class that she expected the students to transgress. Otherwise, why the stern warning? It was this class in which more students touched the toys.

101

Obviously there will be times when it is appropriate for you to check on students, to keep an eye on things, etc. But you may keep in mind the principle of the self-fulfilling prophecy: That which we expect to come true is very likely to come true because we expect it to come true.

RESPONDING TO BAIT

"Hey, Ms. Barker, do you go out on dates? Do you have a boyfriend?"

"Mr. Sontag, what's your first name?"

Can you remember wondering if your teachers had a life outside the classroom? Many teachers try so hard to be very impersonal in classrooms (to protect themselves from ridicule or an imagined loss of respect) that students often wonder if they are human or normal in any way. Occasionally a student cannot resist and his or her curiosity emerges.

How should teachers respond to such questions about their personal life? This depends very much, of course, upon the relationship the teacher has developed with the students. If the relationship has been a fairly friendly one on the whole, then there is less need for defensiveness and less likelihood that students would exploit personal information for their own fun. The following possibilities, however may be kept in mind:

1. The more you resist, the greater will be the curiosity and the harder they will persist.

2. The more impersonal and officious you are, the less likely you will be to develop an effective helping relationship with students.

Of course we are not suggesting you disclose all the details of your personal life with students as a matter of routine. Yet one must have some response when the questions arise.

Your response might be guided by the following:

1. You may want to be <u>friendly</u> with the student and understanding of his or her curiosity.

Example:

"Mr. White, what's your first name?"

Mr. White puts his hand on the student's shoulder, walking away with him. "Lord, you kids are worse than the FBI. Before long you're going to know more about me than my own mother. I guess you think we teachers aren't human, eh? Well, I know we sure seem that way at times, Joe, but, well, I like to be a bit more businesslike in school and keep my mind on helping you learn more. Do you like your name, Joe?"

Notice that the teacher was quite friendly and understanding with Joe. There was very little defensiveness in the response.

Contrasting with that response is one from a teacher who was quite defensive and often <u>unfriendly</u> with students.

"My first name is <u>Mr</u>. Now mind your own business and get to gym before you're late!"

2. You may want to be a little more personal with the student and disclose more, but at the same time try to relate to <u>more</u> than the specific information requested - discuss the related <u>general</u> issue.

Example 1:

A junior high girl asks her young female teacher if the teacher has a boyfriend.

"Yes, I have a boyfriend. His name is Don and we met just last summer. You know, Dawn, I wonder about how lonely it must be for people who have no real friends. Sometimes I wonder what a <u>real</u> friend is too. Do you think we ought to talk about what it means to be a good friend in class sometime?"

103

Notice here that the teacher was friendly and nondefensive and understanding; and that she also chose to disclose some personal information and relate that specific information to a larger issue--friendship.

Example 2:

A high school student asks his teacher about his first name:

"Oh, I don't really like my first name. Do I have to tell you," the teacher says playfully. "It's George--very old fashioned, I guess. You know, I even read about a study once that showed how teachers actually gave lower grades to students who had unusual or unpopular names and how kids usually didn't want to be with other kids whose names were unpopular. Do you think that happens here, Alan?"

Again, the teacher disclosed the information to the student and related it to a larger issue--the significance of unpopular and uncommon names.

3. You may feel that the information requested is really too personal to discuss and consequently you may indicate that you prefer to be friendly with your students but that students aren't really close friends.

Example:

A sixth grade student asks his teacher if she sleeps with her boyfriend.

In a nondefensive, straightforward manner the teacher says:

"Tony, I like to be real friendly with you kids, but questions about a person's very personal life are not for school or students, okay? Now I'd like you to get to gym on time today. By the way, did you get your assignment completed?"

EXERCISE:

Now for each of the following situations formulate an appropriate response based upon the suggestions to allude to a more general issue and to be friendly.

1. A ninth grade student asks you if you ever go to "singles bars."

   "
   _____

   _____

   _____ "

2. A fourth grade student asks you if you smoke cigarettes.

   "
   _____

   _____

   _____ "

3. A sixth grade student asks you if you ever drink liquor or wine.

   "
   _____

   _____

   _____ "

4. A tenth grade student asks you if you ever smoked marijuana.

"_____

_____

_____"

Unit References

Gnagney, W. J. Motivating classroom discipline. New York: Macmillan Publishing Co., 1981.

Weber, W. A., Roth, L. A., Crawford, J., and Robinson, C. Classroom management: Review of the teacher education and research literature. Princeton, NJ: Educational Testing Service, 1983.

UNIT SEVEN
CALMING AN ANGRY STUDENT

A teacher once wrote about an incident in her high school classroom. One of her larger, tougher looking students seemed angry with her. Because of his loud, verbal behavior and profanity she reprimanded him firmly. Upexpectedly the student rose from his seat and began walking slowly toward her. "You want to do something about it?" he muttered. The teacher looked around the room and every student was silent and apprehensive. She wondered what she could possibly do. Should she run? Should she ask others to help? Should she threaten him more firmly? Just as the student moved closer the assistant principal appeared miraculously at the door.

Incidents of this kind are quite rare in schools, but you may want to consider how you might handle such a problem should one ever arise. Effective communication in a situation such as this is more than helpful--it is critical!

Of course, there will be other situations in which a student may be somewhat enraged: a student who has been picked on by another and who now feels the urge to retaliate and the corresponding emotion, a student who receives a failing grade on his report card and storms into your classroom after school.

Whatever the situation, you have to make use of your wits, but you may keep in mind the following:

1. When someone is extremely upset it is usually necessary to deal with the emotion instead of the topic. This means, for instance, a teacher would attempt to calm a student before explaining why she gave him a failing grade.

2. Getting the student (or parent) to sit down may be extremely helpful. It is difficult to be physically harmful from a sitting position.

3. When it appears that the behavior the student has in mind is violence toward you, both of you will benefit if the student can perceive an alternative behavior. For example, a teacher would suggest that the student sit in a chair in front of his desk and tell exactly what he is thinking.

4. Use the salesman's "foot-in-the-door" technique. Ask the student to comply in some small way and he is more likely to comply with further requests.

Example:

   To two students fighting a teacher says, "Ken, take your hands off him" instead of "Both of you go straight to the office."

5. Threatening behavior is likely to further arouse hostility. Unfortunately, a natural response for a teacher, especially a male teacher, is to respond in turn with even greater threat. It is important to remember, however, that to invite hostility in order to show the student who is tougher is hardly professional. Instead the aim of your response should be to de-escalate the problem, not to heighten nor aggravate the situation with a show of strength. Consequently, your behavior should be non-threatening and should serve to calm the student. Non-threatening behavior in such a situation would mean:

   A. Lowering your voice and speaking in a calm tone.

   B. Lowering and relaxing your arms and hands so as to appear nonthreatening.

   C. Making no threat of punishment.

   D. Avoiding touching the student (unless you have a very good general rapport).

   In addition, your verbal response should communicate some understanding and reassurance.

A teacher who reprimands a student who was about to fight with another sees the boy becoming very angry and perhaps explosive. The teacher relaxes and lowers his hands and quietly says, "Andy, I can see you're mad. I know you feel things have been unfair. Please sit down and later I'll see if we can talk about it." The student calms down slightly but still stands. "Please sit at your desk, Andy, and I'll see that I talk to you later. Please sit down." (If the other students are all working the teacher may show indirectly that she now expects the student to sit down by walking away to help other students.)

Notice that the teacher:

1) Spoke quietly and calmly.
2) Avoided arguing with the student.
3) Quietly repeated her request that the student sit down.
4) Mentioned that she noticed the anger he was feeling (demonstrated empathy or understanding).
5) Mentioned that she would deal with him fairly and attempt to hear him out (but only after he sat down).
6) Avoided threats of punishment.

EXERCISE:

Answer the following questions.

1. Why is it suggested that you lower your hands and your voice when responding to an angry or potentially violent student?

_____

_____

_____

109

2. Is it appropriate to relate to the topic of concern (such as the student's assertions about another's behavior) or is it appropriate to relate primarily to the student's feelings and to what it is you want him to do immediately? Which?

_____

_____

Read the following account of a teacher who allowed herself to be drawn into an argument with a student.

A student suddenly rises from his seat and moves threateningly toward another who he accuses of bothering him.

Teacher: "Jim, sit down. If you had been sitting at the right desk he never would have bothered you in the first place."

Jim (loudly): "I'm going to smack his head for him if he opens his mouth again."

Teacher: "Jim, I've seen you bothering other students ten times more than he ever bothers you. Now sit down."

Notice that the teacher keeps giving the student something to react to. She keeps the dialogue going and adds fuel to the burning fire. The dialogue continues:

Jim: "I'll bother him. Just let him open his big mouth again."

Other Student: "Oh you think you're so tough."

We leave the rest to your imagination.

A teacher following the suggestions offered earlier would have responded as follows:

Teacher (moderate voice): "Jim, look at me." (most probable gain, foot in the door) "I can see you're really mad right now. Please sit down and I'll come around and listen to you in a minute."

110

Student: "He'd better watch his mouth."
Teacher: "Please sit down, Jim, I'll be over to get the
story straight in a minute. Please sit down now."
(She goes to help another student, keeping an eye on the
others.)

UNIT EIGHT
WHEN THINGS GO RIGHT - PRAISE

Almost all teachers know rather intuitively that praise is an effective reward and motivator. From a rubber stamp "smiley face" to a "job well done" teachers employ praise generously. Perhaps (can it be?) too generously?

We hope to show you in this section that 1) praise is used in very different ways in different circumstances; 2) that some types of praise are ineffective and often quite damaging; and 3) that some types of praise are effective.

I. Praise is often used in different ways according to whom the teacher is talking.

In his book, Inviting School Success, William Purkey (1978) cites surprising evidence that underachievers actually get more praise from teachers than their more highly achieving classmates! But the form of praise one group gets is quite different from that praise directed at the other group. A teacher directs rather general and meaningless praise to the underachieving students ("That's nice, Joey. Keep working"), while the more highly achieving students receive more concrete, specific praise ("I like that sentence, Rich. Can you add some descriptive phrases to it?").

Why do teachers do this? Many researchers believe that teachers form expectations of students differentially according to their initial perceptions of the student's ability. Brophy and Good (1974) studied teacher behavior relative to students for whom the teachers had high or low expectations. The low expectation students were criticized more than twice as often as the high expectation students, and the students for whom the teachers had high expectations received praise nearly three times as often as low expectation students. Research by Robert Rosenthal and Lenore Jacobson (1968) seems to indicate that students gained less intellectually than others if their teachers were made to believe (by falsified I.Q. reports) that these students had less potential than others. If students do less well because their teachers thought (wrongly) that they had less potential, then we must conclude that teachers are doing something (or not doing something) with these students that they are doing with others of whom they expect more. Perhaps this is the key to why teachers praise underachieving students more meaninglessly: they don't believe that there is anything really worthwhile in the student's work to praise concretely!

EXERCISE:

For each of the following expressions put an ACH on the blank if the student receiving the praise is likely to be an achieving student, and use UNACH if the praise is more likely directed at an underachieving student.

_____ 1. "Beth, you really put something into these kicks. I've never seen your legs so straight."

_____ 2. "That's good, Kathy. You sure do like gym don't you."

_____ 3. "Good, Pete, good. You're coming along just fine."

_____ 4. "Jim, you're essay was very well organized. I could easily follow the relationship between your ideas."

FEEDBACK

Students in situations 1 and 4 are probably more highly achieving and are receiving very concrete, specific praise. The praise in 2 and 3 is rather general and meaningless and probably directed at more underachieving students.

II. Praise which is aimed at the student's personality or character is seldom effective and is potentially damaging; thus we avoid praising the student's character directly.

114

Danny is a sixth grade boy and was the last student leaving his classroom for lunch. As he passed the teacher's desk he noticed a dime on the floor and picked it up, making a great show of his discovery and desire to hand it over. He said, "Look Miss Thompson, I found a dime on the floor. You better take it. I don't want it." The teacher replied, "Well Dan, it's really encouraging to have such an honest person in my class. I wish more of my students were as honest as you, Dan."

Now why would a student make such a show of handing over a dime he found? Perhaps Dan has been stealing from people in school. How would he cope with his guilt and with his fear of discovery and with his need to be accepted? Perhaps the best way to cope would be to take an easy opportunity to make a great show of honesty. This act of "undoing" is intended to put others off guard and to fool even his own conscience.

How does the teacher's response make him feel? Very likely if he has little regard for this teacher he feels that he's put one over on her. In such a case does the praise do any good? If he does feel positive about this teacher, however, he is likely to feel somewhat more guilty than before and he most certainly will feel that this teacher whom he likes so much has a totally wrong perception of him. "She thinks I'm honest--really honest--and... she just doesn't know. God, if she only knew."

Furthermore, if the student is very upset at the discrepancy he may need to do what we will call setting the record straight: he may later make an obvious show of stealing so that the teacher will catch him and know just what (in his mind) he really is.

This act of setting the record straight is not uncommon. In his book, Between Parent and Child, Ginott (1965) recalls the experience of a family on vacation. The mother and father were sitting in the front seat with their young daughter between them. A son slightly older was sitting in the back seat. After riding several hours in relative quiet the mother turned to her son and told him what a good boy he had been all this time. A moment later the boy emptied the contents of an ashtray over the front seat! Why? Just moments before his mother's _general_ praise (good boy), the boy had been thinking of how he would do away with his sister who was occupying the space between his parents--the space he wanted. Consequently, in order to live with himself and to avoid having to live up to his mother's grand expectations, he had to _set the record straight_.

In some situations, however, the child has no opportunity to set the record straight by demonstrating that he or she is really human and capable of behaving less than perfectly. In such a case when the child has no chance to set the record straight what is he or she left with?

A teacher was beginning to decorate her room for holidays when a student stoppped by after classes and offered to help. The teacher and student worked for an hour and a half. When they finished, the teacher said: "Well, Ellen, that's done. My, you're certainly a good worker. You must really be a help to your mother. I'll bet she's glad to have you around."

In actuality Ellen very seldom does _anything_ at home and complains whenever she has to do even the smallest job. Like many children, however, she does enjoy working for other people now and then. The teacher's remarks now leave her in a peculiar situation. She has worked with this teacher for an hour and a half and now the teacher thinks she is the world's most ambitious woman and greatest gift to parents while in fact she is not anything like that at all.

In such a case the girl has no real opportunity to set the record straight (she will probably not feel inclined to run amuck in the room, ripping down all the decorations), so she is simply left with the feeling that she would be wholly worthless and disappointing to the teacher if the truth were known.

Again, this teacher aimed her praise at the character of the student and thus violated the principle we are explaining: avoid praising the student's character directly.

To more fully understand the negative effects of praising the person or his character directly, imagine someone saying all the following to you and imagine how you would feel as they continue (especially if the remarks seem undeserved).

"Boy, you're really nice looking. You have a fantastic complexion. Don't people just fall all over you? You're so intelligent too. Gosh, I wish I were more like you. You really...well...you're just so..."

Would you hope they'd stop? Would you feel like "crawling under a rug," getting away from it? Of course, you'd probably feel a little flattered, but no doubt that would be mixed with embarrassment; and the longer this went on the more you'd feel this discomfort.

EXERCISE:

Now just to understand what not to do or say, try your hand at this very inappropriate form of praise. For the following situations write some comments to praise the student and his or her character or personality directly.

1. A fifth grade student, Kay, sings a song for you which she made up.

"_____

_____"

2. Ron, a ninth grade boy, finally wins a game of checkers against another after losing several.

"
_____

_____ "

III. Instead of praising the student's character in general terms (as you were asked to do above), we refer more appropriately to specific behavior or achievement, or to specific consequences of the behavior, and thereby we allow the <u>student</u> to draw the positive inference about his behavior from our evidence.

In the example presented above where a boy picked up a dime and made an obvious show of being "honest," the teacher more appropriately would respond:

"Well, thanks Danny. Someone must have dropped that dime and now if they come back looking for it I'll have it for them. Maybe they won't have to go without milk. I'm glad you found it."

Here the teacher provided realistic and substantial reason for the boy to conclude on his own, "Hm, I guess I did something good."

The teacher didn't compliment the student unduly. The teacher also avoided praising the boy's character. Because she was not talking in glowing terms about the <u>boy</u>, he could stand there and listen without feeling embarrassed, without wishing she didn't have a misconception about him, without wishing he didn't have to live up to her ideas about his "angelic" character. And he didn't have to set any records straight. From the teacher's concrete <u>evidence</u> of his positive behavior, he could now draw inferences himself about the worth of this small act.

118

EXERCISE:

Read the following story and indicate whether the first or second teacher response is more appropriate.

After school one day a teacher decides to change her room around. Several boys are still in the room and she asks them to help move some heavy bookcases and file cabinets. One of the boys is particularly smaller and underdeveloped compared to the others and he struggles with the file cabinets. It is clearly harder for him to move the furniture. The teacher notices this and says, aside from the others: (put a check mark on the response more appropriate)

_____ Teacher Response 1: "Those cabinets are heavy, Steve. I'm glad you were all here to help. I couldn't have moved those myself. Now the room is the way I need it."

_____ Teacher Response 2: "I didn't know you were so strong, Steve. See, you're getting stronger every day. One of these days you'll be bigger than all those other guys."

FEEDBACK

Clearly the first teacher response provides the student with evidence about which he can substantiate an inference he can make himself.

In the first situation the teacher said, "Those cabinets were heavy" and the student could then infer "Well, I have some strength."

In the second response the teacher says, "You're strong, Steve" and Steve is likely to think, "Who's she kidding."

Again the skill is: <u>Avoid complimenting the student. Instead say something specific that enables him or her to draw an inference about him or herself.</u>

The teacher who got so much help with redecorating her room and told the student what a wonderful worker she was could have said: "Ellen, the room is beautiful. Boy am I glad that's done. If I hadn't had your help I'd have had to come in early tomorrow. Now I can sleep a little later. I just hate to get up so early. Gee, I think all the students are going to like the way the room looks."

Notice that the teacher said <u>nothing</u> about the girl. She referred instead to the <u>effects</u> of her help and the girl could now infer, "Well, I guess I was useful."

EXERCISE:

For each of the following situations write a response which does <u>not</u> speak to the student's character but which rather indicates the positive effect of his or her behavior.

1. You notice a student has taken a lot of time to help another student with her multiplication tables and you want to offer some recognition of that effort.

"_____

_____"

2. A student in your class rather often asks the others to quiet down. Because of this some others have picked up their share of the responsibility and often ask others to quiet down. Now you want to recognize this assistance.

"_____

_____"

3. After a recreation period on the playground a student goes out of his way to help you carry equipment in.

"
_____

_____
                                              "

4. A student who usually puts forth little effort submits a
   short story you find very interesting, enjoyable and well
   written.

"
_____

_____
                                              "

5. You notice a student in your school cafeteria shares her
   lunch with another somewhat unpopular student who has
   forgotten her lunch.

"
_____

_____
                                              "

At this point you might think about how this principle can
relate to your present interaction with others. While we are
primarily interested in the applications of these skills in
schools, it is very likely that practicing these skills <u>now</u> will
establish them as good habit.
Example:
   A young couple had friends to their apartment for dinner
   one evening. As everyone began to eat, one of the guests
   began complimenting the cook. "This is terrific, Jill.
   You're a good cook, Jill."
Of course it was Jill's inclination to shun the praise, "Oh, I
just followed the recipe."

A guest who was a little more effective as a communicator would have avoided general praise directed at the cook (what if she had simply bought the food from the frozen food counter?). Instead he would have said something that would allow the cook to draw the inferences:

"Jill, I'm having some friends over one of these days and I'd love to know how you prepared these."

"Can I have a second helping, Jill. I can't resist."

"This meat and the sauce are delicious. I'm glad I didn't eat much lunch today."

In other words, it is better to compliment someone indirectly.

Not--"You're a great cook!"

Rather--"This is delicious!"

Not--"You really have talent."

Rather--"How did you ever get that effect?"

Not--"You're a wonderful homemaker."

Rather--"I feel so comfortable in your house."

A college student who shares her apartment with a normally very messy roommate returns home one day and finds the apartment cleaned and exceptionally neat.

"Boy, does it ever feel good to come home to this. I kind of wish my parents would stop by."

No comment was directed at the roommate, but the inference is easy for the roommate to draw: "It makes her feel good and she really notices and appreciates what I did."

EXERCISE:

For each of the following situations, write a response to indicate in specific terms how the person's behavior affects you or makes you feel--so that the person can draw a positive inference about what they did.

1. One of your teachers has provided a very worthwhile course experience for you.

   "_____

   _____"

2. One of your parents has given you a great deal of support and sacrificed considerably for you.

   "_____

   _____"

3. A friend has given up a whole day to help you move from one apartment to another.

   "_____

   _____"

Several important research studies have discovered additional factors which make praise effective or ineffective. Stevenson (1965), for instance, found that the more praise was used in a child's home, the less effective it was as a form of reinforcement in a laboratory learning task. Thus, a teacher might best avoid using praise too generously.

EXERCISE

Brophy (1981) reviewed the extensive research on praise and formulated a set of guidelines for using praise effectively. Some of these guidelines are listed below with two expressions of praise after each. Place an "X" before the one which relates best to the guideline.

Effective praise . . .

1. is delivered contingently (after or because of some achievement) not randomly.

    ____ a. "Good work, Sue; Keep it up, Tommy."

    ____ b. "Your model is all done and it's so accurate, Kelly. You even have the Corinthian columns."

Effective praise . . .

2. specifies the <u>particulars</u> of the accomplishment and is not global in nature.

    ____ a. "Your skirt has an absolutely straight hem, Jan, and those pleats are all perfectly even."

    ____ b. "Your skirt is <u>beautiful</u>, Jan. I'm really impressed."

Effective praise . . .

3. is often unique to the specific of the accomplishment, not trite or common.

    ____ a. "I've never seen a project with live animals, Ken. You've really put some work into this."

    ____ b. "Good work, Ken. Very nice job."

Effective praise . . .

4. rewards <u>completed</u> or <u>accurate</u> performance (which has met a standard), not mere participation.

    ____ a. "You spelled ever word correctly, Ben. You get 100%."

    ____ b. "Keep up the good work, John. You have a good start."

Effective praise . . .

5. provides <u>information</u> to students about their skill, not just their <u>status</u>.

_____ a. "Mary Kay, you've done the best in the class. You're way ahead of the others."

_____ b. "Bill, your story had very believable characters, and that really adds to a plot."

Effective praise ...

6. relates to the student's work for its value to the individual and not to how it compares to the work of others.

_____ a. "You got 85% on this test, Jill. That's better than most of the students. A lot of the others haven't done this well on any test so far."

_____ b. "You really improved here, Trish. You're getting to be a much better speller, and your poetry writing should improve now. I know how much you enjoy working with poetry."

Effective praise ...

7. is aimed often at <u>note-worthy</u> <u>effort</u> or success at tasks <u>difficult</u> for the student.

_____ a. "Ted, this project must have taken a great deal of work. It's so intricate and complex.

_____ b. "Donna, you have another great spelling paper this week."

Effective praise ...

8. attributes success to effort and ability, not ability alone or luck, and implies that similar successes can be expected in the future.

_____ a. "Your studying really paid off, Tammy. You got 21 questions correct. You can really do well when you put in that study time."

_____ b. "Jan, you really did it this time. You sure do have the knack for math."

Effective praise ...

9. helps students enjoy the task for their own reasons, not the teacher's reasons.

    _____ a. "Bob, I'm glad you handed in that paper. You'll get full credit now."

    _____ b. "Jenny, you can be proud of this paper. You must have wanted to do well on this work and you did."

Effective praise ...

10. fosters a value for task relevant behavior and does not intrude or distract from task relevant behavior.

    _____ a. "Tom, you worked hard on that, and you have almost every detail correct."

    _____ b. "Alan, see if you can't do as well on the second half as you've done on the first half."

FEEDBACK

The praise most related to each guideline would be as follows:

1. b	2. a	3. a	4. a	5. b
6. b	7. a	8. a	9. b	10. a

Check your work

EXERCISE

Read these expressions of praise now, and write beneath each the guideline above which applies. Write the guideline statement, not just the number. (More than one guideline might apply. Find the one which best applies.)

126

A. "Karen, the table you constructed has been finished with the right materials for the work. You have created an artistic and functional design and the size seems good for various uses."

Guideline "_____

_____ "

B. "You've obviously put a lot of work into this, Eric. You took a lot of time in perfecting this paper and it shows. This kind of diligent thought can get you a lot of understanding in social studies."

Guideline "_____

_____ "

C. "Carol, the improvement you've made with your violin must really be gratifying to you. I imagine you feel you can work your way to a recital before long."

Guideline "_____

_____ "

Unit References

Brophy, J. Teacher praise: A functional analysis, Review of Educational Research. Spring, 1981, Vol. 51, No. 1. Pgs. 5-33.

Brophy, J. E. and Good, T. L. Teacher-student relationships: Causes and consequences. New York: Holt, Rinehart and Winston, 1974.

127

Ginott, H. Between parent and child. New York: Avon, 1965.

Purkey, W. Inviting school success. Belmont, CA: Wadsworth Publishing Co., 1978.

Rosenthal, R. and Jacobson, L. Pygmalion in the classroom. New York: Holt, Rinehart and Winston, 1968.

Stevenson, H. W. Social reinforcement of children's behavior. In L. P. Lipsitt and C. C. Spiker Advances in Child Development and Behavior, Vol. II, New York: Academic Press, 1965.

UNIT NINE
COMMUNICATING ON PAPER

A great amount of the total communication process in schools occurs on paper. Teachers make assignments, students turn in assignments, and teachers return assignments. Inevitably, something is communicated to the student by the teacher in this process. What a student sees on his returned papers affects his learning, his attitude about learning, and his motivation for working on subsequent assignments.

Inevitably, students make errors on their papers. Their writing is immature and often improper. We could hardly expect perfection. Teachers often have thirty papers to grade at a time and our inclination is to search for something to mark.

Have you ever worked hard on a paper, submitted it with some pride and anticipation and then had it returned with red marks on every line? How did you feel or how would you feel in such a situation? Would you be eager to write for this teacher again? Did you ever write a long paper and have it returned with no comment except "Very good, C+?"

The comments you write on a student's paper should serve one or more of these purposes:

1. They may teach the student something she obviously does not know; that is, they may correct misconceptions (e.g.--the correct spelling of a word).

2. They may motivate the student to learn more, to work more eagerly on another assignment.

3. They may inform the student of the rationale for your evaluation.

MAKING CORRECTIONS AND CRITICIZING

It is generally best if a _small_ number of mistakes are marked for correction. If a student makes six different kinds of errors it is probably best to point out only a few on any given paper. In other words, don't feel compelled to mark everything.

If a student misspells the same word six times on a paper it is only necessary to mark the first instance or two.

It is a good idea to mark these few errors with a checkmark (√) or underline, then explain the correction on the back of the paper, or on a separate sheet you attach to the student's paper.

Thus, if five words are misspelled on one side of a paper you would check or underline two or three; then write on the back of the paper: "Jim, you need to learn to spell these words: 1) athlete, 2) masculine, 3) Olympics. Please write each one three times here and resubmit." Or, if a student runs his sentences together you would underline the place where one sentence should end and on the back of the paper or on a separate sheet write: "Denise, you run sentences together. You need to end a sentence with a period and begin a new one with a capital letter: 'The Indians were fierce fighters. They had great courage.'"

PRAISE AND PERSONAL COMMENTS

One of the most effective forms of communication on student papers is the use of personal comments in reaction to student ideas. Many teachers have noticed that students wait anxiously for papers to be returned when they know the teacher often includes personal reaction. One can see the students search for these comments as though they were dollar bills pasted to the paper.

What we mean here by the use of personal comment is any comment that relates what the student has written to the teacher's own experience or thought or opinion. Using these personal comments in a reaction to the student's writing creates a dialogue between student and teacher, and many teachers find it amazing to learn how well this approach motivates many students to submit papers to their teacher.

Below are three excerpts from student writing. Note the teacher's personal comments in the margin.

A. Here the student is writing about her family.

I have two brothers. One is seventeen and one is younger than me, he is eleven. Having two brothers is a pain sometimes because they always loss you.

I had two sisters who were just as bossy when we were your age.

B. The second example is a science project report.

I put stakes around one group of mums and covered these with cloth every day at 5:00 from August 25 to October 1. the other groups didn't get covered. only some of the mums that got covered bloomed earlier

— I really love mums. I wonder why they all bloom at different times.

C.   The third excerpt is from a student's book report.

> The book I read is the Outsiders by S. E. Hinton. The book is about one group of kids who called themselves the greasers and another group who they don't like and about friendship and love. I liked the book because it was real and the feelings were real.
>
> _ We had groups like that in our school. I always wanted to be in one. I felt a little lonely, I guess.

It is not necessary to make personal comments for every paragraph; nor is it necessary to avoid all critical remarks. But if you habitually include personal remarks and keep your criticisms and corrections limited to a small number and explain on the back of the paper, then you'll notice how effective your paper communication is in motivating students to work.

EXERCISE:

Now read the following student essay with these points in mind and react appropriately. That is, write personal comments in the margin and provide criticism as suggested. No grade is necessary.

How to study and take tests

On last Friday Mr. Carlson held a meeting for everyone who wanted to go to it on how to study and take tests. He teached us about how we should have a good place to do our homework; about how we should have a regular time each day and not all at once, like the day before its due.

He said that a good place to do your homework is in your room; if you have a desk and a good lamp or at a table if the T.V. isn't on. He said you should that you should do your work at the same place all the time and not do anything else their like eat or anything.

The SQ3R method
is one he teached us too.
About studying textbooks.
the way you do it is
you skim over the pages.
Find the pictures and the
subleads and read them.
then your suposed to make
some questions you think you
can answer. If you read the
chapter. Then you read a
little bit only a few
paragrafs and you recite
out loud ov to yourself
what you read and you
cover up the parograf
while you do it. Then you
go on and do the whole
Chapter the same way. Read
a few parographs and
resite what you learnt.

UNIT TEN
COMMUNICATION FOR DEVELOPMENTAL AND INSTRUCTIONAL PURPOSES

I. <u>RESPONDING TO CHILDREN'S QUESTIONS</u>

A father and his daughter were riding on a subway train.

"Daddy, what makes the train go?"

"The engineer runs the train."

"What's an engineer, Dad?"

"He's the man who makes the train go."

A sixth grade student asks his teacher a question:

"Miss Ash, why don't we get to change classes in the sixth grade like they do at the junior high?"

"That's just the way it is, Cindy."

An eleven-year-old boy asks his father how gasoline makes a car go:

"Well Don, the gas is pumped into what we call combustion chambers--hollow cylinders inside the engine--and a spark plug gives off a spark at the right time to create an explosion in the cylinder which forces a piston down. Now the pistons are all connected to a shaft which turns because of the up and down motion of the cylinders and the shaft turns the rear axle. That's it, Don."

Each of these situations has one thing in common--the child's question leads to absolutely no mental work on her or his part. In the first situation the child is quieted with a brief, meaningless answer. That child now is satisfied with the simple response and the case is closed.

In the second situation the child is given no answer at all and led to believe, in fact, that there is no answer to the question.

In the third situation the child's curiosity is satisfied with a brief and straightforward answer which again allows the child to conclude "case closed." Nothing more to wonder about. Nothing more to do.

Contrast the responses in the situations above to the following situations:

A child eating dinner with her parents asks a question:

"Mom, what's 'retarded' mean?"

"You've heard this word at school?"

"No, Jill said her brother is retarded and he acts--well--kind of funny."

"You mean his behavior is different?"

"Well, he has funny eyes and he doesn't talk right."

"I guess his mind and body are different, eh?"

"Yeh, does it mean he's dumb?"

"Well, can you think of a way we could learn about retarded people or the word retarded?"

"We could look in the dictionary."

"Okay, here the dictionary says.... Now, how can we learn what it is like, I wonder?"

"We could ask Jill. She might know."

"Maybe you could talk with her tomorrow."

Now read this dialogue between a teacher and his student:

"Mr. Balles, is it true that Christopher Columbus didn't discover America?"

"You've heard that someone else did, eh?"

"My mom said it was really some other guy, some Viking."

"Maybe everyone's believing that Columbus was the one and it's all wrong if it was this Viking--that would be strange, huh?"

"Well, I always heard it was Columbus."

"Well, how are you going to clear this thing up, Sam?"

"Well, can I go to the library?"

"Sure. Right after the spelling test. But you'll be missing this film I'm showing."

These last two situations are markedly different from the first two interactions. In these last two examples a mother, first, responds to her child's question about the meaning of the word <u>retarded</u> in such a way as to encourage the child to do his own mental work on the problem. Note that the mother didn't say "Look it up in the dictionary, dear." While the child is doing his own work with that approach, it does not provide the kind of guidance necessary for engaging the child's curiosity and motivation.

Instead, the mother seemed very <u>interested</u> in the question (and its background). Then she helped the child think of <u>resources</u> for learning. No doubt this mother would remember to ask later about what the child had learned.

The teacher in the last dialogue also avoided giving a pat, matter-of-fact answer. Instead he expressed some interest in the question and helped the student to become even more aware of his curiosity and his motivation and he helped the student think about action that could be taken toward a resolution of the question.

Responding to children's questions with pat, matter-of-fact answers seems quite natural to us as parents and teachers. Yet, far more than simply acquiring information, a valuable goal of education is developing an active sense of self-as-learner, and a skilled logical mind. An old Indian saying expresses the point well: "Give a man a fish and he can eat for a day; teach him to fish, and he will eat the rest of his life."

Teachers can indeed give students bits of information but far more valuable is acquiring the motive, ambition, willingness, need and interest in acting upon one's felt questions. Thus, with such a view, students are learning subject material and they are learning to learn.

THE SKILL--Respond often to students' questions so as to leave the student more interested and to leave him with a greater awareness of resources for resolving the question on his mind.

This skill requires that you often leave the question unanswered. You will be leaving the student "hanging." This open-ended guidance often tends to make the student even more motivated toward her question; and your help in developing awareness of resources enables the student to move forthrightly toward learning on her own.

Many years ago B. Zeigarnik (1927) designed an experiment which demonstrated that students could better recall unfinished tasks they had begun earlier than other tasks they had completed earlier. This implies that problems not brought to closure stay with us and motivate our perception (we "keep an eye out" for material relating).

Now, read the following dialogue between a student and a teacher and note in the margin what the teacher is doing.

138

	"Miss Avery, why did the Vietnam War get started, anyway?"
Teacher clarifies question	"You wonder what caused it, Ann?"
	"Well, yeah, I mean why should we have gotten involved in a country so far away?"
Teacher heightens motivation	"About fifty thousand Americans died in that war, Ann. How did such a thing ever get started. I guess that's what you want to know."
	"Wars seem so dumb, don't they."
Teacher evokes thinking about learning	"They seem so stupid and yet there must be some reason. Do you have an idea, Ann, about how you might learn about this--the reasons for such a war?"
	"I thought maybe I could do my book report on a book about it."
Teacher offers follow-through guidance	"Can I help you look in the library at lunch, Ann?"
	"Okay."
Teacher offers another resource	"By the way Ann, I believe Mr. Spencer has a Master's Degree in Political Science. He ought to know something about this."

EXERCISE

In the space below write a similar dialogue as it might occur between you and a student when you are trying to stimulate the student toward learning-on-his-own with guidance.

Use one of the following questions as a start:

"Mr./Miss _____, why do some leaves turn yellow and some turn red?"

"Mr./Miss _____, why doesn't it get cold in Florida in the winter?"

"Mr./Miss _____, are we really going to have all solar energy by the time we are adults?"

Now begin with the student's initial question:

Student: "_____

_____"

You: "_____

_____"

Student: "_____

_____"

You: "_____

_____"

Go on as far as necessary.

_____

_____

_____

_____

_____

_____

_____

_____

AN IMPORTANT NOTE: SOME QUESTIONS NEED NO ANSWERS

We were working here with questions the student was sincerely curious about. Often, especially when you are alone with the student, a question will be asked as a "cover" for more personal concerns the student would like to talk with you about. If you proceed slowly and somewhat non-directively, then the student will sense that he can take the dialogue in a more meaningful direction if that is what is on his mind. However, if you jump at the chance to provide guidance toward the student's specific question and rise to your feet and lead the student to the library, the student will sense that you are only interested (at the moment) in teaching as opposed to listening. Usually questions which serve as "covers" are not of the inquiry type anyway. "Cover" questions are more often as follows: "Mr. Jenkins, what page did you say our homework was on?" or, "Heh Miss Donald, where'd you get all those plants?"

II. RESPONDING TO WORDS, PHRASES, EXPRESSIONS TO STIMULATE INTELLECTUAL ACHIEVEMENT

Expansion--Vocabulary Stretching Responses

There seems to be mounting evidence that human (especially adult) language directed at the child is a critical factor in intellectual development. This evidence relates most generally to young children, but there can be little doubt that all of us benefit when hearing new vocabulary, the meaning of which is made clear to us.

The skill involved in expansion or vocabulary stretching is simply to rephrase, as often as possible, the student's expression into 1) a slightly <u>expanded</u> expression, and/or 2) a similar expression using different vocabulary.

In the following examples the teacher <u>expands</u> or stretches the young child's expression.

A. "Mr. Coddle, Joe has my truck."

"Joe has that big, old, heavy metal truck has he?"

B. "My crayon broke."

"Your crayon split right in half?"

C. "I'm making a pumpkin, Mrs. King."

"You're drawing a big, round, Halloween pumpkin for us?"

The value of expanding or stretching the student's utterances are twofold. First, the child hears time and again that there is more than one way to express anything. Second, the child learns over and over that simple expressions can be enhanced.

EXERCISE

On the blanks below each child's expression write a corresponding <u>expansion</u>.

A. "Tommy has a water pistol, Mr. Watkins."

"_____

_____"

B. "I ruined my picture."

"_____

_____"

C.   "I have new shoes, Miss Kaufman."

"
_____
_____
                                          "

The skill related to expansion is that of offering different vocabulary for the student's expression. This means that the teacher merely rephrases what the student says using vocabulary perhaps slightly advanced. Note the following examples:

A.   "I lost a tooth, Mr. Green."
     "You shed that tooth, eh Robert?"
B.   "Cheryl is always late."
     "Yes, she's often tardy."
C.   "Can I be the weatherman today, Miss Thompson?"
     "Okay, Ken, you can be the meteorologist today."

EXERCISE

Rephrase each of the following expressions with vocabulary different and possibly more advanced.

A.   "I think I want to be a teacher when I grow up."

"
_____
_____
                                          "

B.   "I can't do anything right today."

"
_____
_____
                                          "

C.   "This is hard, Mrs. Allison."

"_____

_____"

An interesting approach for venting one's emotion on children and at the same time stimulating their language development is related to the use of I-messages. The technique is to shower the child with words that vividly describe your feelings (I messages).

> "John, when you leave paste on your desk I just become livid."
>
> "This shouting in class is unfair. It's an outrage to my sense of justice.
>
> "Why, I'm so happy, Glenn, I'm feeling downright euphoric."

Often a child will hear such an expression, look up at you and say, "What's euphoric?" Then you can tell her.

EXERCISE

For each situation below write a response which expresses your emotion with one or more words the child is not likely to understand at first.

A.   A student has been cutting paper and has clippings scattered all over the floor in the back of your classroom.

"_____

_____"

B. Your class has been studying American government and a student surprises you with a model of the White House which obviously took many days to build.

"
_____

_____
                                              "

C. A student who has been absent for several days returns and you wish to express some happiness in her return.

"
_____

_____
                                              "

Analogy Responses

Teacher: "Can someone tell me what is wrong with this statement: The sun goes down each evening?"

Student: "Well, the sun doesn't go down, actually; the Earth turns."

Teacher: "Yes. Look, this ball will be the sun and this ball will be our Earth. See, darkness comes to our side when the Earth turns each day. The sun remains still. When we think the sun goes down it's like thinking a ship has fallen off the Earth because we don't see it shortly after it has left port. Why are these two thoughts similar?"

Student: "Because in both of them we're like fooled by the way things look."

Teacher: "Yes, it looks to us like the sun goes down; and it looks to us like a ship doesn't exist anymore when we can't see it. In fact we are fooled in both situations because we can't get off of the Earth--way out there--and see everything at once.

The teacher has demonstrated the use of analogy in teaching. That is, the teacher helps students understand one idea better by showing another similar idea and how the two relate. This technique quite often enables students to understand a principle or concept more meaningfully because they very likely are aware of the nature of the idea used as analogy. These students were no doubt aware that a ship disappearing over the horizon does not fall off the Earth and yet they understand how easy it would be to be fooled by the phenomenon. Relating the idea of the sun "going down" to the idea of the disappearing ship enables the students to better understand. Now read the next example:

Student: "Mr. Denton, our book says that people are prejudiced because they want a scapegoat. Does that mean like they want to have someone to blame things on--like they want to have someone to put down?"

Teacher: "I guess that's sort of like when you have a real bad day--you need to take it out on others huh?"

Student: "Yeah, I guess it makes you feel better to put down someone else when you're...well...when things aren't going right for you."

Here the teacher showed an analogy between social prejudice--a difficult and abstract concept--and classroom scapegoating, a concept the student knows all about.

In the next example the teacher asks for an analogy to be developed by students.

Teacher: "Now we have learned that plants use energy from the sun to produce chlorophyll and then to give off oxygen. Does that remind you of anything? Can you think of something very different from a plant that operates this way... Perhaps the word plant would be a clue."

146

Student: "Oh yeah, a factory, and we call a factory a plant."

Teacher: "How is it similar, Tim?"

Student: "Well, the factory uses electricity or gas or something to like make rubber or steel to make products and they give off...pollution!"

Here a teacher again asks students to think with analogy:

Teacher: "We have studied some causes of wars. One was the problem where one nation needs something or wants something very much which another country has, such as seaports. Can anyone think of something aside from actual war which would be similar?"

Student: "Yeah, like some other guy has a real neat girl and you really want her and a 'war' starts between you and the other guy."

Again, these students may better understand why a possible cause of war is greed--because they have seen the analogy with a very real adolescent situation.

The value of using analogy in teaching comes through providing an association between a new concept and one the student already knows. Consequently the teacher explains how one concept or principle is similar to another and then explains the similarity. "A familiar analogy puts unfamiliar subject-matter into a recognizable language so that it can be clarified and organized" (Joyce & Weil, 1972, pp. 235-236).

Teacher: "Yes, sometimes we call the land outside the cities and towns the country but that word is also used to mean our whole nation.

"This is similar to the way we call Ohio or Florida a state and also use that word to mean a whole nation."

Explanation   "In both cases we use a word for a larger general area to represent a smaller area within it. Even the principal has an <u>office</u> within "the office."

On the blank beside each numbered item, indicate the letter corresponding to the appropriate analogy:

____ 1. The brain
____ 2. Jet propulsion
____ 3. Layered clothing warmth
____ 4. Study carrel
____ 5. Sound waves moving through water better than air

a. Air space between window paines
b. Blinders on a horse
c. A computer
d. Voices carrying over wire vs. atmosphere
e. Released balloon

EXERCISE

For each of the following situations develop an analogy and explain the similarity to students. Remember, you are attempting to explain something to students by comparing this to something they already know:

A. You are explaining the network of interstate highways and the way they are connected such that traffic flows freely from one artery to another.

B.   You are explaining the reason why the earth is dark on one side when light on the other.

"
_____

_____

_____

_____
                                                     "
_____

C.   Your students are studying about how cities and towns developed around natural harbors (places where goods were readily available to meet common needs).

"
_____

_____

_____

_____
                                                     "
_____

A much more thorough and creative model of teaching metaphorically has been developed by William J. J. Gordon (1970) for use in classrooms. His strategy for "exploring the unfamiliar" involves several possible steps.

1.   The teacher provides some explanation of a new topic.
     Example: Mr. Evans briefly explains the way in which the sun remains in one place and the earth rotates, causing darkness and light on different sides of the earth.

149

2. The teacher communicates an analogous situation and asks the student to describe it.

   Example: Mr. Evans describes a ship going out to sea and asks his students what happens to the sight of the ship from port.

3. The teacher asks the students to put themselves in the place of the analogy--to be the analogy.

   Example: Mr. Evans asks the students what they would see if they were on the ship. What would they think the people who were left behind would see.

4. The teacher asks the students to identify points of similarity between the original idea and the analogy.

   Example: Mr. Evans asks the students how the perception of a ship "disappearing" is similar to the view he explained of the sun "disappearing."

5. The teacher has students explain where the analogy does not fit--what is not similar.

   Example: Mr. Evans asks students to state how these two situations are not alike.

6. The teacher moves back to more explanation of the original topic.

   Example: Mr. Evans further explains the relations between a person at one spot on the earth, the earth itself, and the sun.

7. The teacher asks students to develop their own analogy for the new concept.

   Example: Mr. Evans asks the students to think of any other way we are fooled by having an incomplete view of the situation.

EXERCISE

Now, see how well you can compare some topic or idea you might be teaching to some similar topic or idea. Take the lesson through Gordon's seven steps.

Idea or principle to be taught.

_____

_____

_____

Step 1. Provide some explanation of the idea taught.

"_____

_____

_____"

Step 2. Communicate an analogous situation and have students describe it or explain it.

"_____

_____

_____"

Step 3. Ask the students to put themselves in the place of your analogy (use the specifics of your example).

151

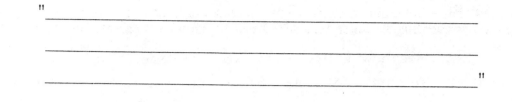

Step 4. Ask the students to identify some points of similarity between your analogy and the idea you are teaching.

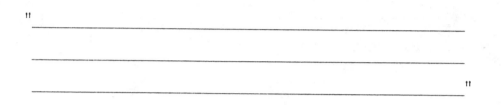

Step 5. Ask the students to say how the analogy is not appropriate.

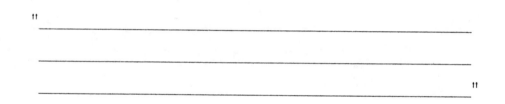

Step 6. Proceed with further explanation of the concept being taught (briefly here).

Step 7. Lastly, ask the students to suggest another analogy for the idea taught.

"
_____
_____
_____
                                                "

III. QUESTIONING

Kinds of Classroom Questions

"Okay, who remembers the nations in the European Common
     Market?"
"Class, what is the name of the process for converting coal to
     gas?"
"Tony, can you tell us the three largest states in America?"

All of these questions have at least one thing in common.
They require simple recall. They require almost no mental
work on the part of the student. Either one knows the answer
or one doesn't, and unfortunately there seems to be clear
evidence that these factual level questions are the kind most
frequently asked by teachers.

If the purpose of education is to help students develop
intellectual skill, our questions should stimulate the student's
mind toward more than a "search" for stored data. Questions
of a more developed nature can stimulate the development of
associations and connections, an awareness of application and
utility of ideas and a sensitivity to relationships among elements
of a concept. Certain kinds of questions also can arouse student interest and motivate students to learn.

Using Bloom's Taxonomy of Educational Objectives (Bloom,
et al., 1956), the following hierarchy of types of classroom
questions can be derived.

153

1. <u>Knowledge Level Questions</u>

   These are questions which ask for simple recall of literal or very factual information.

   Examples: What is the capital of Michigan?

   Who was the first U.S. astronaut?

   What is the numerical value of π ?

2. <u>Comprehension Level Questions</u>

   These questions call for some interpretation on the student's part and require answers which reflect a meaningful understanding of an idea as opposed to literal or verbatim recall.

   Examples: What would another term be for a state capital?

   What would be another acceptable name for the European Common Market, one which would reflect its function?

   What, in your words, is meant by the statement: For every action there is an equal and opposite reaction?

   What are some examples you can imagine of imperalism?

   Notice that with a Comprehension Level Question the student is often translating or putting ideas into other words, or giving appropriate examples she has not previously associated with a concept.

3. <u>Application Level Questions</u>

   This question form calls upon students to demonstrate the utility of ideas or information or to make appropriate application of a principle.

Examples: Can you think of three people in different situations who would be effected by the principle: For every action there is an equal and opposite reaction?

What would the value of $\underline{x}$ be in the equation $4x = 24$?

What would a chart of our population growth over the past thirty years look like?

4. Analysis Level Questions

Analysis questions probe the student's understanding of relations among elements in a whole. They call for an ability to see the way in which one part of a whole affects another.

Examples: Suppose the major character in this novel had not been a man. How would the story be different if it had been a woman?

How do you imagine the Civil War would have gone had General Grant been appointed much earlier?

What would be the effect if we disconnect the catalytic converter from this engine?

5. Synthesis Level Questions

These questions call upon students to go beyond recognizing and understanding relations (as in Analysis Level), and ask students to create something from certain elements (a theme, play, problem solution) and to bring learning from various areas together.

Examples: Now that we have studied so many
revolutions, can you develop some
categories of revolutions or civil
wars?

Using what you have learned about
human prejudice and scapegoating, can we work on a stage
play to reflect this human tendency?

As you know, schools categorize
students according to age. Can
you come up with a different
logical plan for grouping students
in schools?

6. Evaluation Level Questions

Evaluation Level Questions are by far the most demanding to answer adequately. They assume a
thorough knowledge on the part of the student and
require considerable judgment. They generally ask
students to appraise or compare material, to draw
conclusions, to criticize, to interpret, etc. All of
this requires the student to have mastered the
material under consideration (and likely the related
material as well).

Examples: Now having studied ecology for a
whole semester, compare these
two essays on ecology for tho-
roughness and accuracy.

Which play do you believe better
explains the development of the
Vietnam War?

What are the major fallacies made in
this essay?

EXERCISE

Using the explanations presented above, try to identify the level of each of the following questions. Write one of the following on the blank beneath each question: Knowledge, Comprehension, Application, Analysis, Synthesis, Evaluation.

1. What is the definition of a molecule presented in your text?

   _____

2. Who is the father of atomic physics?

   _____

3. Using the conversion formula, how many kilometers would a car travel in one and one-half hours at 54 miles per hour?

   _____

4. What was Lincoln basically trying to say in his first inaugural address?

   _____

5. For some time we have been studying about the American Revolution. Can you now describe your idea of how a film about the American Revolution should depict the American leaders?

   _____

6. What, in your own words, is happening when we drop the solid cylinder into the water?

   _____

7. What do you think would have been different had Werner von Braun and other leading German physicists gone to the Soviet Union instead of coming to the United States?

   _____

8. In what ways was the play "1776" accurate and in what ways was it inaccurate as a reflection of the American Revolution?

   _____

FEEDBACK

Although it is improbable that everyone would agree totally on categorizing these questions, your answers would at least agree with the author's if you responded as follows:

1. The first question which asks the students to state a definition is a Knowledge Level Question. It requires only <u>recall</u> and memorizing. Generally any response from memory would be to a Knowledge Level Question. On the blank below, write an example of a Knowledge Level Question.

    "_____

    _____"

2. Recalling the name of anyone would of course also be for a Knowledge Level Question. On the blank below write another Knowledge Level Question.

    "_____

    _____"

3. Converting data from one form or value to another using mathematical principles or a conversion formula would best be categorized as for an Application Level Question. The question involves a practical problem for the student to apply what was learned about conversion to metrics. The question presents a problem to solve and as such is an Application Level Question. On the blanks below write an Application Level Question.

"
_____

_____
                                            "

4. Asking what Lincoln was trying to say is like asking
   for a personal translation of Lincoln's message. As
   such the question is a Comprehension Level Question.
   Such questions usually require the student to articulate the meaning of something without resort to an
   exact definition. These questions often require the
   student to explain something in her or his own
   words. Below write an example of a Comprehension
   Level Question.

"
_____

_____
                                            "

5. Asking students to develop an idea or description of
   how some complex event could be represented in a
   structured format would best be categorized as a
   synthesis task. The student must create some new
   product from previous learning or from diverse fields
   of study. On the blank below write a Synthesis
   Level Question.

"
_____

_____
                                            "

6. Asking students to <u>explain</u> what happens when a solid
   enters a liquid is probably best categorized as a
   Comprehension Level Question. The student is asked

to explain some phenomena accurately without resort to the wording of a formal law or definition. The student was not given any practical problem to work on (Application Level), nor was the student asked to explain specifically the relations among events in a process (analysis). Below write a Comprehension Level Question.

"_____

_____ "

7. Responding to a question about potential differences, events and history due to a different migration of German scientists requires a thorough understanding of the relations between those scientists, the events they created and events which followed. This question then is at the Analysis Level. Analysis Level Questions typically ask students to specify effects from a change in some part of a pattern. On the blank below write an Analysis Level Question.

"_____

_____ "

8. This question which requires students to criticize a play in terms of historical accuracy is an Evaluation Level Question. Such questions require a thorough familiarity with the subject and are the most demanding. On the blank below write an Evaluation Level Question.

Curiosity Arousing Questions

Some teachers have found rather motivating effects from writing a particular kind of question on their blackboard before a lesson or on a study guide before a text section to be read. These questions termed <u>Curiosity</u> <u>Arousing</u> <u>Questions</u> (Bull & Dizney, 1973) relate specifically to material to be studied and contain <u>discrepant</u> <u>elements</u>. Something in the question just seems not to fit.

Examples:

A. In what ways does the manufacturing of missiles create a greater climate of peace?

B. In what ways can praising a child be damaging to your relationship with that child?

In the first example the idea of manufacturing missiles certainly seems discrepant with the idea of peace. In many ways they just don't go together. This discrepancy is potentially felt as a curiosity by the student and he is then motivated to resolve this perceived problem by reading or attending to your explanation.

In the second example the student is presented with a question which suggests that praise may be associated with a negative response from a child. Most people believe, of course, that praise is a very positive and appropriate behavior which always affects the relationship positively. Yet, as you have learned, certain forms of praise are not effective. The strange form of this question again sets up a sense of curiosity in the student which she or he works then to resolve.

Other examples of curiosity arousing questions would be as follows:

What do we call the female hormones found in males?

What "crops" do ants raise in their underground farms?

In what ways do rooftop gardens create a city farmer? Note that in the last two questions certain words are combined to make a single discrepant idea: "underground farms" and "city farmer".

EXERCISE

Write two or three curiosity arousing questions below. Each should have terms which seem discrepant. Imagine, of course, that your students are going to be reading material which explains the discrepancy or that they would be attending to a lesson.

_____

_____

_____

Ways of Asking Questions

Teacher: "Okay class, who can tell me why Shakespeare put the gravedigger scene in Hamlet?"

John: "To add to the death symbolism?"

Teacher: "No, no, someone else? Cindy?"

Cindy: "Because people really wanted or liked gory stuff like that. It would attract people--like violence in films today."

Teacher: "Oh, come on class, someone else."

This teacher is on a fishing trip--fishing for correct answers. The teacher very likely has a "correct" answer in mind and he will go from one student to another until some lucky student comes up with what the teacher wants.

This emphasis upon fishing for correct answers has several effects:
1. It discourages participation from anyone who doubts her answer.
2. It discourages participation from anyone who would feel bad about being wrong.
3. It encourages guessing at the expense of reasoning.
4. It potentially produces false pride for students who are good guessers.
5. It fails to stimulate reasoning.

An alternative to this tendency to "fish" for correct answers is the practice of probing for reasoning. When a teacher probes for reasoning, no answer is right or wrong. The teacher is not concerned (for the moment) with the correctness of the student's response. She is interested in creating a stimulus for reasoning. With this approach, any student can participate.

Teacher: "What purpose does the gravedigger scene serve in Hamlet? Ron?"

Ron: "It makes the characters seem more human and the audience would identify with them easier I guess."

Teacher: "Do you recall anything from the textbook that leads you to say that, Ron?"

Ron: "Um, ah well, they said that uh these plays were mostly about royalty and that the people didn't really live like royalty--but more like the gravediggers."

Teacher: "Ah, so you assume that Shakespeare felt he needed to increase a sense of identity. Does someone else have another idea based upon anything else in the play notes? Pat?"

Pat: "Well, they said that the play uh needed relief or something--that it couldn't be so heavy all the way through."

Teacher: "What did you read to lead you to say that, Pat?"

Pat: "Well, in the notes they said that--let's see, it's here somewhere... 'Comic relief seems to keep the audience from becoming emotionally overloaded and adds contrast.'"

Teacher: "That section then leads you to assume that the scene was added for those reasons. What about Ron's idea, Pat?"

Notice here that the teacher was interested more in creating an opportunity for the student to think and reason than in getting a correct answer. The teacher responds in the same way whether the student seems to be right or wrong. Basically the teacher ignores the correctness of the answer at first but concerns herself or himself with the student's reasoning process. What assumptions is the student making? What does the student base his thinking on?

Read the following example:

Teacher: "Now if we learn that nouns are words which can take plural and possessive inflections, would the word nation be considered a noun in the sentence, 'The nation is in trouble'?"

Dan: "Yes."

Teacher: "Why do you consider it a noun, Dan?"

(Notice that the teacher resisted the temptation to jump ahead with the lesson at this point when the student offered a seemingly correct answer.)

Dan: "Well, you could say <u>nations</u>."

Teacher: "Meaning?"

Dan: "Well, like you could say nations are sovereign states."

Teacher: "And, yes, that makes the word a noun, but why?"

Dan: "Because it's a plural form, more than one nation, you know."

Teacher: "So, Dan says <u>nation</u> is a noun because it can take a plural form. Would you reason the same way, Debbie?"

Here, the teacher demonstrates that even a correct answer can be temporarily ignored for greater attention to underlying reasoning.

EXERCISE

Now write a dialogue between a teacher and a student where a teacher asks a question and the student responds and the teacher probes not for correct answers but for reasoning.

Wait-Time

As a final note to our discussion of questioning skills, we must point to an amazing phenomenon in classrooms. According to clear research evidence (Rowe, 1977) teachers typically wait no more than approximately one second for a student to respond to a question! This tendency is no doubt related to the "fishing" habit and the tendency is certainly inappropriate where we have an interest in encouraging students to participate in thinking and reasoning. Only simple, memorized responses can be generated in seconds. Reasoning takes time.

In reference to questioning, we call the time necessary for thinking wait-time. Simply put, when a teacher poses a question for a student or for the class, she or he will appropriately wait silently until a student is ready to respond. We are all somewhat uncomfortable with silence following a question; yet, this moment of silent wait-time stimulates students to think (Sund, 1971). When the teacher constantly rephrases the question or calls upon student after student, no one can really concentrate.

Classroom Recitation

When a teacher calls upon students to answer questions in classroom groups, should she follow a random pattern or should she call on students in ordered turns?

Imagine yourself in a classroom, each student has a workbook, and the teacher is calling upon students to answer questions from various section of the workbook. The pattern the teacher is using is one of ordered-turns. He begins at the beginning of each row and works back. You can predict when you will be called upon.

Now, change the situation in which you imagine yourself. The teacher is now calling on students randomly - you can't tell when he might call on you.

In which setting would you feel more anxious? In which would you be more likely to pay attention?

Although random recitation has long been assumed to be more effective than the ordered method (Gnagey, 1981), some evidence has been found to indicate that it is better to call on students in ordered (predictable) turns (Anderson, Evertson, Brophy, 1979). This has been explained partly with the notion that when teachers call on students "randomly" they actually call on students selectively. That is, they call on certain students quite often and they call on others very seldom.

A way around this problem would be to place each student's name on a separate card and shuffle the deck before starting. Call on each student as her card comes up and reshuffle the deck each time. Thus you avoid biasing your questioning and use a more truly random pattern. Of course, you may try the ordered-turns approach and find that it sometimes works better. You might even ask the students which they like better (or which method they would use if they were teachers).

Unit References

Anderson, L., Evertson, C., and Brophy, J. An experimental study of effective teaching in first-grade reading groups. Elementary School Journal, 1979, Vol. 79 (4), pp. 193-223.

Bloom, B., et al. (eds.). Taxonomy of educational objectives. Handbook I: Cognitive domain. New York: McKay, 1956.

Bull, S. G. and H. F. Dizney.   Epistemic-curiosity arousing pre-questions: Their effect on long term retention. Journal of Educational Psychology, 1973, Vol. 65, pp. 45-49.

Gnagey, W. J. Motivating classroom discipline. New York: Macmillan Publishing Co., 1981.

Gordon, W. J. J. The metaphorical way of learning and knowing. Cambridge, Mass.: Synectics Education Press, 1970.

Joyce, B. and Weil, M. Models of teaching. Englewood Cliffs, N.J.: Prentice-Hall, Inc., 1972.

Rowe, M. Questioning. Phi Delta Kappan, (Summer) 1977.

Sund, R. B. Growing through sensitive listening and questioning. Childhood Education. November, 1971, Vol. 51, pp. 68-71.

Zeigarnik, B. "Das erledigten und unerledigter handlungen." Psychologische furschung. 9, (1927): 1-85.

EPILOGUE

Again, we refer to that bumper sticker: COMMUNICATION IS VITAL TO LIFE. Strangely, so many things constantly vital to life are more or less taken for granted. Because we breath the air around us constantly and need it vitally, we never give breathing a thought. With food it is often the same. How <u>considered</u> is our nutritional life? Communication is something we have been doing since infancy, non-stop! What difficulty there is then in attempting to pause and consider, to study, to practice and polish those communication patterns. Yet, because communication is the professional tool of any teacher, the tool can only be professional with consideration, training, practice, evaluation, and care.

Aside from gaining specific skills through this learning experience, perhaps you also have a far greater appreciation for the differences in communication patterns, for the different effects of different communication patterns, and for the necessity to keep those patterns of communication in schools highly professional. If you have this appreciation to complement the skills achieved through the hard work you have committed to this workbook, then we have reached our goal!

TO THE STUDENT OR TEACHER

Now and then some student or teacher will take the time to tell me about the effect of using some skill or other that he or she has learned from these pages. Then, the work I have put into this project is rewarded. I feel at those times that this person and I have really worked together. If you have found some special effect from using any ideas from this workbook, I would enjoy hearing from _you_. Your questions and suggestions are also welcome. Just write to me - Dr. Richard Burke, Department of E.D.F.I., College of Education, Bowling Green State University, Bowling Green, Ohio 43403. Then you and I can work together.

ABOUT THE AUTHOR

Dr. Richard Burke teaches in the College of Education at Bowling Green State University. He taught junior high school language arts for five years, worked as a high school counselor, and served as second president of the Midwest Association of Teachers of Educational Psychology. Dr. Burke has three children.